Do You Really Get Me?

Do You Really Get Me?

Finding Value in YOURSELF and OTHERS
through Empathy and Connection

JOSEPH SHRAND, M.D.
with Leigh Devine

Hazelden
Publishing

Hazelden Publishing
Center City, Minnesota 55012
hazelden.org/bookstore

Library of Congress Cataloging-in-Publication Data

Shrand, Joseph, 1958–
Do you really get me?: finding value in yourself and others through empathy and
connection / Joseph Shrand, with Leigh Devine.
      pages cm
   ISBN 978-1-61649-588-6 (paperback)
1. Self-perception. 2. Self-consciousness (Sensitivity) 3. Empathy.
4. Interpersonal relations. I. Title.
   BF697.5.S43S477 2015
   158.2—dc23
                    2015019805

Editor's notes
   The names, details, and circumstances may have been changed to protect the
privacy of those mentioned in this publication.
   This publication is not intended as a substitute for the advice of health care
professionals.
   Alcoholics Anonymous and AA are registered trademarks of Alcoholics
Anonymous World Services, Inc.

19 18 17 16 15   1 2 3 4 5 6

Cover design: Jon Valk
Interior design and typesetting: Percolator
Developmental editor: Sid Farrar
Production editor: Heather Silsbee

To Russell Haddleton, JD, who spent his life reminding others of their value, making him one of the most valuable people I have ever known. I miss him dearly.

And to my cousin Myron Gelberg, a gentle giant who never had an unkind word for anyone, and always saw the value in others—not always easy as he lived in New York City his entire life. I miss him as well.

CONTENTS

FOREWORD

Most of us are obsessed with others and constantly seek their thoughts and feelings about ourselves, real and imagined. These are the flesh and bones of the thoughts and feelings we have for ourselves and the ever-playing background music against which we live our internal lives. We attribute these self-thoughts and self-feelings to ourselves, but the tools of thinking and internal language that we use are very much external to us. These are tools acquired in our life histories of *inter*-action, our experiences with others turned inward.

These internal thoughts and feelings may be joyous at times, and miserable at others; they can bring us to moments of exhilaration, or moments of deep despondency; they can promote a sense of belongingness in the world, or they can isolate us in the shadows of mental illness. What is clear though is the notion that the thoughts and feelings we have for ourselves cannot be separated in any way from the thoughts and feelings we have for others. Were we able to nurture a positive approach to one, the other should follow. This may be a helpful piece of advice to all those struggling with hurtful self-thoughts and self-feelings, but actually this notion is much more than that. This notion goes deep into the biology of our species, into the earliest development of our minds and brains, and into the deepest fabric of our culture and personal well-being.

Nothing shaped the brain of primates more strongly than sociality—the fact that we live together. Nothing shapes the behavior of an infant more strongly than the eyes of her caregiver; and nothing shapes the behavior of a caregiver more strongly than the smile of her infant. In the history of our species and in our own individual histories, this reciprocal social interaction occurring between baby and caregiver, this ever-expanding mutually reinforcing choreography, is the platform for brain development, and for the ever-increasing sophistication in our ability to communicate with others and with ourselves.

From visually seeking the movement of others—in their bodies, in their faces, in their eyes—to attributing intentions and feelings, thoughts and beliefs to others, we go from the utter fragility of a newborn to a sophisticated theorist of the minds and hearts of others. In so doing, we become the social world around us, and the world around us is painted and sculpted by the world within us. Biology, our self-referential world of feelings and thoughts, the presence of those closest to us, and the social world beyond become one and the same. Elucidating those connections is a key aspect of contemporaneous evolutionary biology and social neuroscience. But equally if not more importantly, this is also every person's individual quest. Knowingly or unknowingly, this informal and internal "research" we are all engaged in is what so much of our happiness, or unhappiness, depends on.

So comes this book you have in your hands. In straight prose and using a beautiful web of illustrations, Joseph Shrand and Leigh Devine begin to make these connections explicit, clear, approachable, and, most of all, personal. Knowing these connections brings about empowerment and promise. Knowing the genesis of our self-thoughts and self-feelings gives us a bridge to the process of learning and internalization. This bridge also brings us closer to control: knowing "what" is a big step toward knowing "how." But the very process of making connections to others as a way of feeling more connected to oneself; of extending compassion to others as a way of feeling more compassionate to oneself; of easing off on the perennial routine of judging others as a way of becoming more accepting of oneself—therein, in these various processes, lies the wisdom of this book. And with it a modality of therapy and self-help that highlights, at times in a visceral fashion, the profoundly social nature of our hearts and minds.

Ami Klin
Director, Marcus Autism Center, Children's Healthcare of Atlanta, and Emory University School of Medicine

ACKNOWLEDGMENTS

Sid Farrar, my editor from Hazelden who recognized the simple power of the I-M Approach from the minute he heard about it. His encouragement helped bring Theory of Mind to the general public.

Linda Konner, whom I remind repeatedly, and shout to the world, that she is the best agent ever.

Leigh Devine, MS, my writer and friend who has always been able to take our books to the next I-M.

Julie Silver, MD, my first editor at Harvard without whom I would never have become a writer of books at all.

Tony Komaroff, MD, who has championed getting the message of science into the hands of the general public.

Ora Gelberg, Myron's surviving wife, whose practical and pragmatic view of the world has never ceased to amaze me.

Avrom Weinberg, PhD, for pushing me to explain. He is very, very missed.

All of my clinical and support staff at CASTLE who have embraced the I-M Approach as the foundation of treatment. Our adolescent patients never feel judged or devalued, allowing them to explore why they do what they do as an agent for change.

Jim Quine, my "brudder from anudder mudder," who grasped the power of the I-M Approach the first time he heard it about a decade ago and is using it in public schools to help students with special needs. Jim shows how easy it is to turn these children from seeing themselves as less than they can to the best that they can.

Kim Fisher, my program director, who has embraced the I-M Approach to treat teenagers challenged by drugs and alcohol by helping to simply remind them of their value.

Erich Englehardt, my student who continues to challenge me as I refine the I-M Approach and its application.

Jerry Fain, truly "faintastic," who prompted me to write essay after essay on the power of the Approach.

Jeff Brown, PhD, who has never lost faith despite one unthinkable challenge after another.

Charles Darwin, need I say more?

E. O. Wilson, right up there with Darwin.

The insights of Alan Watts on the application of Eastern philosophy to Western science and our universal interconnection.

My parents, Hyman Shrand and Frances Shrand, who always, always saw me as able, valuable, and encouraged me to be creative and think outside the box.

My wife Carol's parents, Richard and Dorothy McCann, who helped bring into the world that one amazing, unique person who has never doubted me, and for all their love, support, and belief.

Lana Maxwell, my sister who still sees me as her little brother: an I-M I will never escape!

My sister Susan who left us all too soon.

My kids, Sophie, Jason, Galen, and Becca who showed me how a child is always influenced by the four domains, and how influential a parent can be in creating an environment in which a child can demonstrate who they are. Each of them has enlightened me about Theory of Mind and entranced me as it emerged in them. I hope they know their value to me, and how valuable they are.

Brendan Mulhearn, his recently departed mother Mickey, and his alive and kickin' Aunt Ginny, whose spirituality and grace are founded in truly, truly seeing the value in every one. Brendan, I am impressed!

Elizabeth St. Lawrence, my sister-in-law, who was one of the first people I ever showed the I-M Approach way-back-when in 1982; a critical thinker who keeps me honest.

Daniel Mumbauer, president and CEO of High Point Treatment Center, who took a chance on me back in 2008 when he asked me to help design an adolescent addiction treatment program. His mission and that of the I-M Approach have always been in synchrony.

Fran Markle, vice president of High Point Treatment Center, who has given me the support I need to make a real difference in the lives of kids and their families challenged by addiction.

State Senator Vinny Demacedo of Plymouth and Barnstable counties, Massachusetts, and State Representative Jim Cantwell of Scituate and Marshfield, Massachusetts, who use Theory of Mind all the time, every day, bringing a sense of value to the tens of thousands in their communities. They are both truly inspirational to me and I am grateful to call them my friends.

Christopher Sarson, the creator and executive director of WGBH's *Zoom*, my Zoompapa, who taught me all about respect.

Andy Short of ImprovBoston, an amazing educator and improvisor who has helped build the value of our teenagers in Drug Story Theater (DST). Professor Nicole Conlon, who has taken the stories of our Drug Story Theater teens and, with her student Olivia Hughs, crafted them into a brilliant and compelling script. Stacey Lynch, my administrative assistant, who is willing to tackle the most difficult problems to get the show up and running. Michael DuBois and Larissa Farrell who have helped capture the development of the teens' new Theory of Mind as they rekindle their value. And all the kids of DST, including Melvin, Jonathan, Nick, another Nick and his mom and grandmother, Peter, Kyle, Michael and his dad, Shana and her mom, and the many other teens who were willing to share their stories and how drugs and alcohol influenced Theory of Mind in the people around them.

Captain Bob Sullivan, my flying friend cut from the same bolt of cloth. It is remarkable how our views converge, always with the foundation of respect. From way up high he has an overview of how valuable all of us truly are.

Steve Aveson, a truly inspired and inspirational human who has brought the news of the world to millions. In each story he reports, he conveys the respect and value of the human condition.

Professor Ami Klin whose knowledge of Theory of Mind knows no bounds. One of the deepest thinkers I have the fortune to know.

Professor Simon Baron-Cohen who broke open the door on Theory of Mind in his increasingly popular books. I am honored to be on his email list!

Professor Andres Martin, my fellow Fellow from long ago, a brother soul, and one of the true champions of child psychiatry. Andres has never doubted me, always pushed me to clearly articulate what I am trying to communicate, and opened door after door with the generosity that exemplifies who he is. I hope he knows how much I value his friendship and support.

Professor Michael Jellinek, an amazing psychiatrist and leader in the field, and one of my first teachers in child psychiatry. I still remember him telling me in 1993 that I would never forget what was important when listening to a patient. He is right.

Paula Rauch, my supervisor, who once said, "Joe. You are ignorant, not stupid."

Edward Perry of WATD, Marshfield, Massachusetts, a great radio man who has always been willing to pass the megaphone so the message of respect and value can be transmitted to all.

Larry Bosco, one of the most incredible therapists I know who has taken the I-M Approach and applied it for years, even after he left the hospital where we worked together. In fact, for a long time he was the only person I trusted to use the Approach without my direct supervision.

David Singer, a brilliant neuropsychologist who has debated with me the foundations and application of the I-M Approach, always making sense and helping me to move to a deeper understanding and appreciation of the brain.

Carlos Vasquez, a friend and chiropractor who never gets his back up!

The hundreds of innovators and thinkers whose work has inspired me and been integrated into the I-M Approach.

The thousands of patients who have shared their stories and shown me how respect leads to value and value leads to trust. I am honored and privileged to have been of service.

And to my wife, my best friend, the woman who has always, always, always treated me with respect, has valued me, has pushed me to always explore my I-M, and whom I trust without any doubt at all. Thank you, my vitamin C. Thank you, Carol.

INTRODUCTION

It's all in the mind.

—George Harrison

You may be reading this book because you think you are broken in some way and need to fix something in yourself. But what if you were to accept the radical idea that in fact you are not broken at all? What if all you are is curious and maybe even perplexed about how to feel happier, better, and more valued in a community or society that can often seem cold, unfriendly, and alienating? We all experience loneliness, rejection, even alienation within our own family or social groups at times. When this happens, we want to feel more connected to others, but have we already decided that other people just don't "get" us?

If these questions sound familiar, you're not alone. In spite of the explosion of social media and digital networks promising us more connection with everybody, the result has been the opposite for a great many people. You may read three hundred texts and wade through five hundred emails each day, yet you may not have a single human conversation. Digital contact does not equal true connection. If it did, then fewer of us would be turning to prescription medications for depression and anxiety, and well, the opposite is true. I'm a psychiatrist, and the words, thoughts, and fears expressed by my patients, the tears they shed, and the tears they hide remind me of this each and every day. "Shares" and "likes" are nice, but they can never replace visits, voices, hugs, and other symbols of true respect and value.

I'm writing this book because I work in a field where I see people of all ages, cultures, and economic and educational levels who worry that indeed they *are* broken, and being broken, they don't fit in and won't be accepted by the people who matter to them. This worry can even lead to feeling disconnected from humanity in general.

The problem is that we think it's about *us*, that something is wrong with *us*. But when we really delve into our lives and circumstances it becomes clear that our problem isn't *who* we are, but who we *think* we are. We have to deal with problems, challenging events or situations, unhealthy environments, and life obstacles every day. But I believe that the real problem is that we sometime react to these challenges and the world around us from a position of seeing ourselves as broken.

In this book, we'll explore how feeling disconnected from others is very often about self-perception. It's about how our own idea of who we are is projected to the world. This notion may be hard to accept, but we look to others to reveal to ourselves who we are and how we are to act. We do this all the time and are, for the most part, completely unaware of it. Yet, it's a natural condition of being a successful social animal, and it starts from the very moment a mother looks into the eyes of her infant.

When you ask someone you meet, "How are you?" you're not asking that question only because you want to know how that person is doing. On a deeper level, what you also want to know is, "How do you perceive me? Am I OK to you?" The way this person responds to us—through words, tone of voice, and body language—will tell us. If the person is warm, accepting, and appears to regard us with respect, we feel good about ourselves and connected to that person.

But if the person seems dismissive, we often feel rejected, anxious, and "less than." When we get into a pattern of interpreting people's messages this way—whether our interpretation is accurate or not—and this feeling of rejection persists, then we can start to feel broken. But I don't believe that anyone is really broken. What's more likely is that our perspective needs adjustment. We can alter our perception of how people see us. We all have the power to change our perspective and thereby change how we interpret others' reactions to us. And when we discover this ability and the advantages it brings, and we practice it consistently enough, we can come to see our own power to positively influence our family, friends, communities, and our very world.

By reading this book, you're going to learn about our fundamental human need for connection to others—a need as primal as our need for food—and about why it's so important to feel valued by others in order to value ourselves. You're also going to learn how real and meaningful connection happens—and I'm talking about the kind so deep that your brain chemistry actually changes: the real, uniquely human connection that relieves anxiety and gives us the sense of peace, security, and confidence that allows us to feel at home in the world and actualize our dreams.

THEORY OF MIND

So how do we know what others really feel about us? What happens when we say that someone really "gets" us?

I'm going to introduce you to a rather clunky psychological term: "Theory of Mind," or ToM. In short, this is the brain tool that gives us the capacity to appreciate another person's perspective. We know how rewarding it is to feel empathy for another person and to have others empathize with our feelings. This couldn't happen if we didn't have the capacity to "read" other people's facial expressions, body language, and the content and tone of their verbal messages. When we do that, we can make an assessment about what they're thinking and feeling—how they see us and the world—at any given time. This is Theory of Mind.

People on the autism spectrum have a diminished ability

to assess another's thoughts and feelings because their ToM is "turned too low"—or even turned off. But for most of us it's almost always turned on, and we use it constantly and unconsciously. From the moment we wake up and encounter another person, we are using it to assess the other person's perspective and intention, just as they are using their own Theory of Mind to assess ours.

Let's say I'm sitting in a doctor's office and a person comes in after me but gets called in by the receptionist to see the doctor first. Ordinarily this might not bother me, depending on how my day is going or how I'm feeling about myself in general. If I'm feeling good and secure and valued in my life, I'm likely to speculate that the receptionist is having a bad day or is preoccupied—or that she simply mixed up the visit times, and she's distracted and forgot I had arrived first. But if I'm not feeling so secure, I might wonder if she doesn't like me for some reason, or perhaps she likes the other patient better because they're more attractive, interesting, or fun. Of course, I might also think the other person has a more serious illness and should be seen first as a way to make the perceived rejection by the receptionist a bit more palatable.

Think about your own life. At work, a boss's smile and nod of appreciation create a very different feeling in you than a look that suggests disapproval. On a date with someone you enjoy, positive verbal and nonverbal cues from that person create a very different feeling than cues suggesting the person isn't interested in seeing you again. These simple examples show how other people influence us through ToM, just as we influence everyone with whom we come in contact.

Which brings us to one of this book's most important messages: *You control no one, but you influence everyone.*

We use Theory of Mind to interpret subtle and overt cues to instantly assess how another person is thinking or feeling. But what we're *really* wondering is, "What the heck are ya thinking or feeling about *me?*" This distinction is critical. ToM not only enables us to assess the perspectives of others; it also becomes the entry point to *how we see ourselves through the eyes of others*. And how we see ourselves is influenced by how we think other people see us.

The more we understand how Theory of Mind works, the better we can use it to do two important things:

- to positively influence how others perceive us, and, correspondingly,
- to positively influence how others think and feel about themselves.

It feels good to make another person feel valued, as good perhaps as when someone makes *us* feel valuable. We create a feedback loop: the more we make others feel valued, the more valuable we feel—and vice versa. We can do this at any time by using ToM effectively, not as someone who is broken, but as someone who deserves to feel connected to other people.

And the really good news is that we aren't doing this just to make ourselves feel better. When we make the choice to enhance someone's value, we are essentially becoming a benefactor to that person. A person who feels valued not only respects, values, and trusts this benefactor in return but also is much more likely to enjoy life and spread that enjoyment to the world. The best way to truly become a happier person is to help someone else feel the same way. In that sense, this book takes a broader view than a traditional "self-help" book.

I have had the remarkable good fortune to work with people in their time of need. As a psychiatrist, I have met men and women, boys and girls struggling because of how they think other people see them. Some have become so distressed that they feel they have no value at all, and that they deserve any misfortune that happens to them. What I've learned over the last twenty-five years is that deep down, every one of my patients simply wanted one thing: to feel valued by another human being, to feel connection. This book will help you understand this basic, human psychological need, and give you the tools you need to accomplish this goal.

THE I-MAXIMUM APPROACH

Related to Theory of Mind is another important tool: the "I-Maximum Approach." In my previous book, *The Fear Reflex*, I described the I-Maximum, or I-M Approach as a method by which we learn to recognize that each of us is doing the best we can at any moment, given the influence of the world around us, and the world within us. Our I-M is our "current maximum potential." Current: right now. Maximum: the best that we can. We always have the potential to change to a new I-M in the very next second.

I developed I-M as a treatment approach. But it has become as much a philosophy for living, one that helps people remind themselves and others that each of us has value. It's the basis for my belief that no matter how difficult our lives seem at times, it's not because we're "broken." Instead, when we recognize our own value and can see the value in others, we can find the next "maximum," the next I-M, that allows us to face our problems more effectively. In this book, you'll see references to the I-M Approach that will help you gain a deeper psychological understanding of how life circumstances are constantly at play, affecting our well-being and that of every human being, in every moment. As our circumstances change, so do we. We think differently from moment to moment, and we're influenced constantly in four major areas of life:

- the biological domain
- the "Ic" domain (how "I see" myself and how I think others see me)
- the home domain
- the social domain

Let's take a closer look at these areas.

The Biological Domain

Your biological domain relates specifically to your own physical health and circumstances. This domain is not just about whether you have diabetes or high blood pressure. It's also about how you're digesting your breakfast, whether you're sleepy, or whether a new yard tool has given you a blister on your hand. Our brains and bodies are changing all the time, and at each moment they attain a new I-M.

When people say that health is all that matters, they're not kidding. According to the I-M Approach, even when we have physical challenges, we are functioning at an I-M that we must accept in every given moment.

An example: I was invited to give a speech to a group of psychiatry peers last year. I had worked hard developing and writing the speech, but the morning of the presentation I woke up with laryngitis: all that work had to be delivered in a whisper. I was disappointed but understood that in that given moment I was at my I-M, doing the best I could, accepting that I could not control everything.

The Ic Domain

Pronounced "I see," this domain describes how you see yourself combined with how you think other people see you—the total sum of your self-perception in any given moment. The Ic domain is most closely linked with Theory of Mind, and we'll explore that link in more depth later in the book.

An example: Emma knew the answers but was afraid to raise her hand in class. The thought crossed her mind one day that the teacher and the other kids must think she was stupid. That thought ballooned into a dark cloud of self-doubt that crushed her confidence for the rest of the day. A simple negative thought, allowed to spread unchecked—even one with no basis in truth—is all it takes for the Ic (our self-concept) to take a hit. Through the lens of the I-M Approach, Emma came to see that her thought was the best she could do at that current moment, but that didn't mean it was true. She wasn't stupid at all; she just thought at that moment that other people saw her that way. With this I-M insight she could keep valuing herself for all the hard work she put in daily. Perhaps she would find courage tomorrow to raise her hand and be at a different I-M; she could certainly try.

The Home Domain

This external domain refers to our family environment and the people in it. The home domain pertains to our past home and family situation as well as our current one, for this is where we formed many of our ideas, habits, and beliefs as children—patterns that continue to influence us even in adult life. Some people experience deep emotional conflict in their home domains. Others experience warmth, support, and validation. Either way, it influences our Ic domain and the relationships we forge as we grow older.

An example: A young client of mine—let's call him Rick—hadn't seen his father since he was five years old. He'd left Rick's mother and moved across the country. Rick had only heard from him once in ten years. It had always been hard for Rick to see other kids with their dads. He grew to feel that something was wrong with him. He tried to bury his pain by using drugs and alcohol. With work and time, Rick came to understand that what happened in his home domain wasn't his fault. His father's actions did not need to determine Rick's self-concept (his "Ic") and who Rick would become as he grew into adulthood. Hard as it was to accept, Rick began to see that his father also had an I-M, even if it was one that Rick didn't like or condone. Rick became determined to not be like his dad when he had children of his own. He would stick around and remind his children every day of their value.

The Social Domain

Outside of home and family, the social domain is everything and everyone in our environment: at work, at school, at a restaurant, out with friends, or just walking down the street. Since most of us spend the bulk of our waking day in the social domain— often as much or more than the home domain—we experience a broad array of potential issues and challenges that can appear overwhelming.

An example: From day one in her new job, Shawn experienced unprofessional treatment from her direct boss, a man who was a close friend of the company's owner. At least twice a week, his explosive temper erupted at someone's desk, so everyone in the office walked on eggshells. The dilemma for Shawn was deep. She was miserable, but she needed the income and, ultimately, she needed a good recommendation from this job. The firm was well-known in her industry, so it would be a highlight on her re-sume. Making a conscious tradeoff, Shawn was able to put her life and her social domain in perspective by achieving balance in her other three domains so she could tolerate staying in the position for a full year and realize her career goals. She also used the I-M Approach and began to wonder why being mean was the best her boss could do: what was going on in his home or social domain and how did this influence his Ic and biological domains? The negativity of her boss did not mean that she was less valuable at all. With this new perspective, Shawn felt less angry and less stressed. The change in her biological domain rekindled her self-esteem in her Ic domain. The shift in her emotional response helped her be more productive at work, and it ultimately got her an excellent recom-mendation when she did move upward in her career.

This diagram shows how the four domains are interconnected and result in your I-M, your current maximum potential.

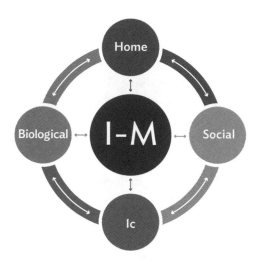

THEORY OF MIND AND THE I-MAXIMUM APPROACH: HOW DO THEY WORK TOGETHER?

As you read this book, you'll become increasingly aware of how you're already using ToM in nearly every single human interaction you have. You'll also learn how to make better use of it. But Theory of Mind is not the destination. It's the means by which you get there. The actual destination is developing the ability to find value in yourself and others. When you start using ToM, you'll inevitably become more aware of how powerfully our human interactions can shape our lives. But the most transformative moments come when we recognize that in any given moment, we—you, me, all of us—are doing the best we can, the best that the circumstances in our four domains will allow.

Thanks to the ever-changing dynamics of our key life domains, we always have the potential to change and reach a new maximum that opens us up to feeling a greater connection with others that in turn increases our sense of value—both our own and other people's.

According to the I-M Approach, real connection is based on respect. When we learn to respect others (and they us), we help fulfill that core human desire to feel valued. Feeling valued leads to trust, and trust is the force of genuine friendship that can connect us all. When we begin to filter life's challenges and our perceptions of other people's perspectives through the I-M, we begin to see meaningful changes:

- We recognize how we're influenced across the four domains: our biology, Ic (how we see and are seen by others), home, and social domains.
- We can see how each domain influences the others.
- We recognize that a small change in one domain can have a huge effect.
- We see that we are more in control of our lives than we thought.
- We can begin to move toward how we want to be seen, and how we want to see ourselves.
- We begin to respect ourselves and can then choose how we want to treat ourselves.
- We recognize that everyone has an I-M, so we control no one but influence everyone.
- We recognize that we are not powerless and can approach life without anxiety.
- We forgive ourselves and others.

As you read the following chapters, you'll be reminded of how life's various circumstances impact the four domains of your own life, and perhaps the lives of those around you. The I-M Approach offers a road map to how each of us can find fellowship, friendship, and meaningful connection to other human beings, and to ourselves.

Where did Theory of Mind begin? In the first chapter, "Harmony: The Evolution of the Social Animal," we'll look at ToM from an evolutionary perspective. Why would ToM evolve at all? And what made it such a successful adaptation that it is now practically universal, the building block of all human interaction?

Sometimes we use ToM to deceive another person. This human behavior is the focus of the second chapter, "Untruth: The Art of Lying." I'm not lying when I tell you that this sometimes innocent and sometimes very malicious behavior can start when we're very, very young. Honestly. White lies are designed to protect someone's feelings—perhaps our own—while malicious lies are meant to take advantage of someone else. The risk of lying is that we'll get caught. It's hard to trust a liar, so we may jeopardize our relationships and alliances, and maybe even lose our membership in the group.

Membership depends on feeling a part of a group—a feeling that depends on Theory of Mind. The third chapter, "Membership: The Need to Belong," digs into how groups are formed, and some of the brain chemistry that binds us together. But just as easily as we can be bound, we can be excluded. This very dark side of ToM is explored in the following chapter, "Alienation: The Price of Not Belonging."

What's the takeaway? All of us can use ToM to help others feel *a part of* the group as easily as we can make them feel *apart from* the group. Both are in our nature. In fact, "Nature: Our Innate Capacity for Choosing Connection," is the title of the final chapter. We all use Theory of Mind intuitively, but applying the I-M Approach makes using ToM a technique. This awareness can complete the bridge between the emotional and thinking parts of our brains. The thinking brain is where ToM lives. The I-M Approach suggests that *respect* is that bridge. Using the vehicle of ToM, we know when others respect us. Feeling respected feels good. That's the result we all hope for when someone else really "gets us." And being truly understood by other people so we have real connection with them: that's what all of us are looking for in the end.

The first letters of the five chapter titles spell out the word HUMAN. Theory of Mind truly defines us as humans in need of belonging, social animals at our core. We're all part of one collective group, one large social domain called humanity. That's why ToM really matters: it allows us to fulfill our optimal I-Maximum as benefactors and valued members of the human family.

1

Harmony

THE EVOLUTION OF THE SOCIAL ANIMAL

The law of evolution is that the strongest survives!
Yes, and the strongest, in the existence of any
social species, are those who are most social.
—**Ursula K. Le Guin**

My first glance at the phenomenon of Theory of Mind in early human development came twenty-five years ago, when my wife Carol and I were driving from Cincinnati to Hartford, Connecticut, in a rented U-Haul truck. Our fourteen-month-old daughter, Sophie, sat between us in her car seat. I had just finished medical school and we were moving east. I was about to begin my psychiatry training at the University of Connecticut's Institute of Living. The drive was about fourteen hours, and to keep Sophie entertained we let her eat lollipops.

After her third lollipop, we were still in Ohio. Concerned about her dental hygiene, I said to Sophie, "No more lollipops." Sophie looked at me, looked at her mother, took a lollipop, and unwrapped it. Then she covered her eyes with her left hand and, with her right, put the lollipop in her mouth. She was sitting right between us, so what was happening in that remarkable, developing mind of hers? After a few minutes, we realized that she thought that if she couldn't see us, then we couldn't see her—specifically, we couldn't see her continue to eat her lollipop. At fourteen months, she hadn't yet fully developed Theory of Mind, the capacity to appreciate someone else's perspective. Sophie kept eating her candy.

But Sophie would *not* have covered her eyes unless she thought we had a perspective about *her*. She covered her eyes so her mom and I would "disappear" and she could eat her lollipop in peace. This is critical to ToM: before we can take someone else's perspective we first develop a "theory" of how the person is perceiving us. From an evolutionary perspective this makes a lot of sense. Millions of years ago it was much more important to know if someone was looking at you as their lunch than if they were hungry. First comes how they see you, and then comes your perspective of how they feel.

Those of us working in the fields of psychiatry and neuroscience have learned that most children progress gradually toward the developmental milestone called Theory of Mind, or ToM. We can't see another person's mind, or the way it works. Instead, we create a "theory," or an idea of what the other person is thinking and feeling, just as we assume they theorize about our thoughts as well. This is a built-in brain function that we ordinarily take completely for granted. For instance, you see a woman standing on the corner waiting for a cab. If it's a cold, rainy night you can theorize how frustrated she must feel as cabs pass her, already occupied. Go a step further with this scenario. You see a man move a few feet in front of this woman and stick his hand out for a cab. You can theorize quite easily how this action will affect the woman's brain and emotions. Your own Theory of Mind is what first makes you aware that this act is inappropriate and even downright aggressive; you can theorize that this act will anger another. Your ToM will also enable you to see how others would perceive the man's action.

The vast majority of people develop this capacity between the ages of eighteen months and five years. Once developed, we use it all the time, so fluidly and naturally it just "happens." In fact, having never heard the term or the idea, most of us are not aware we are using Theory of Mind at all.

But we are.

As social creatures, a fully functional ToM is fundamental to our ability to get along well with other humans in the world. When we wonder if someone likes us, or doesn't like us, if someone is angry with us, if we are admired, envied, despised, loved—that's ToM at work. We "theorize" about the waitress serving us food if there is too long a delay in taking our order, or about the doctor who seems to be taking too long to return to the examining room, or about the person we hope will say yes to a first date. If you ever wonder about such things, then congratulations, your ToM is in sound working order. Throughout this book, you'll learn how to use it to your advantage, but let's first take a look at how we discovered its very existence.

▶ THEORY OF MIND AND EMPATHY

If you ask most people what empathy is, they might have a hard time explaining it. But they will know instinctively how it feels, on both the giving and receiving end. As a basic definition, empathy involves one person's ability to appreciate the emotions another person feels, often from a similar life experience. For instance, if your friend's dog died, and you've also had that experience—or another experience of losing a beloved companion—then you can empathize with his pain and grief, and vice versa. This common experience has the potential to then bind you and your friend together as he recognizes that you understand and care about what he's going through. It calms the brain to know a person really "gets" how you feel.

You feel less alone and more connected when others can relate to your situation.

Empathy is not possible without a foundation of Theory of Mind. The very first step toward empathy is the ability to appreciate on a basic level that another person has thoughts and feelings separate from your own. A person who can't follow the emotional component of communication can't experience or practice empathy. Empathy lets people know that they are not alone, that another person "sees" what they are experiencing. Being seen like this can help a person bear even the most unbearable loss or enhance the pleasure of even the smallest success.

Unfortunately, a person can have ToM and not have empathy. In extreme cases, we're talking about a person who is likely to have sociopathic tendencies, which is fortunately quite rare. In less sinister cases, ToM can be exploited to get us to do things we may not have thought of doing, like buying a warranty on a new computer, or adding on the expensive deluxe sound system in a new car. Really good salespeople can tap into our ToM, not lying to us but exploiting our fears and desires. Has that ever happened to you? Have you purchased something that, in retrospect, you wish you hadn't? At the time it made a lot of sense because your own ToM may have been subtly manipulated by a master!

The concept of Theory of Mind was first presented by two psychologists, David Premack and Guy Woodruff from the University of Pennsylvania. For their groundbreaking study published in the *Journal of Behavioral and Brain Science* in 1978, they investigated whether chimpanzees had the ability to attribute intent or mental state to others. The scientists observed chimps looking at a video of a human actor struggling with challenges such as being locked in a cage, being unable to reach food, or shivering from cold. The chimps were then given photographs of the solutions to each of these problems, and they consistently selected the correct remedy, as if *they* had been the ones locked in a cage, reaching for food, or shivering from cold. Premack and Woodruff showed that a chimpanzee can take the perspective of another animal. The paper was titled "Does the Chimpanzee Have Theory of Mind?"

Humans take other people's perspectives all the time, but it was Premack and Woodruff's work that ushered in a brand-new focus of research: how, when, and why do we develop the ability to assign mental states to ourselves as well as to others? In 1983, University of Salzburg psychologists Josef Perner and Heinz Wimmer built on Premack and Woodruff's work and created tests called "false-belief" tasks for children. One of the classic examples they developed to demonstrate ToM is called the Sally-Anne "unexpected location" task. Children being given this test were told the story of two characters, Sally and Anne. Sally has a basket and Anne has a box. Sally also has a marble. Sally puts the marble in her basket, and then she leaves the room. While she's gone, Anne takes the marble out of Sally's basket and puts it in her box. Soon afterward, Sally returns.

In the test, the child is asked where Sally will look for her marble when she comes back into the room. Very young children typically respond by saying that she'll look in Anne's box—after all, we've just seen Anne put it there. They don't understand yet that Sally would still believe that the marble is where she left it, as she hadn't seen Anne move it. From the young child's point of view, if he or she saw it, then everyone saw it. This was the very same action we witnessed in our daughter Sophie with the lollipops. The young child's perspective is the same as everyone else's, and everyone else's the same as the child's. A child who says Sally will look for the marble in Anne's box has not yet developed Theory of Mind.

Two-, three-, and four-year-old children are just beginning to form ToM, this ability to take another's viewpoint. They don't yet understand that Sally's thinking is separate from Anne's and that their own thinking is separate from everyone else's. At around age five, that begins to change. And by the time children are six or seven, they are more likely to say that Sally will look in the place she left the marble—in her basket. By this time, they are fully aware that other people have their own distinct thought processes and unique perspectives. And crucially, ToM brings with it an ability to predict other people's behavior. This combination of taking another's perspective and anticipating others' behavior is what drives our relationships.

Without thinking about it consciously, most people assume that everyone has the ability to take another person's perspective, to have an active and intact ToM. In fact, we expect others to be interested in what we're thinking or feeling, and to give us a sign that they're interested. When someone doesn't meet this expectation, we tend to think that there's something wrong with him or her or, even worse, that something might be wrong with us. In reality, however, ToM abilities exist on a spectrum. Some people have strong abilities to take another's viewpoint; others less so.

The lack of ToM becomes very obvious, and even uncomfortable, when we interact with people who have *not* developed this ability, who have psychiatric or brain conditions such as autism, dementia, or various types of neurological damage. These people may behave in ways that seem insensitive, lacking in interest or concern for others. But what we know is that these people are not being oppositional in response to our feelings. Rather, they are *oblivious* to our feelings and that we might have any feelings at all. But once we become aware of their lack of ToM, we're more likely to feel empathy for them.

It seems almost inconceivable that humans aren't born with an intact ToM. It's the very underpinning of our human social interaction, something so deeply practiced that we're conscious of it only when we're around others who lack it. Yet, none of us are born with this ability up and running. Like our innate language capabilities, research is just now revealing that ToM begins to emerge in humans around eighteen months but takes at least five years to fully develop.

Theory of Mind is now known to generate from a part of our brains called the prefrontal cortex. From an evolutionary standpoint, this area is considered part of the "new brain" or neocortex, as it's the most recent region of the brain to develop in humans. If you put the palm of your hand on your forehead, your prefrontal cortex is right there behind it. Often called the executive brain, it's where we process incoming information, compare it to the past, solve problems, create plans, and anticipate the consequence of those plans. As such, it has provided enormous survival advantages for humans. Theory of Mind, then, is the application of executive functioning to help "read" the mental states of others, such as their beliefs, desires, and intentions.

In just the last decade, neuroscientists have homed in on the precise region of the brain where our ToM actually develops and resides: the right temporo-parietal junction. Rebecca Saxe, principal investigator at the Social Cognitive Neuroscience Lab (Saxelab) at the Massachusetts Institute of Technology, has been scanning the brains of adults and children using a technique for measuring brain activity called functional magnetic resonance imaging (fMRI). Researchers at the Saxelab have worked with children conducting false-belief tests such as the Sally-Anne task, and they've been able to place kids as young as five in the scanners for brain evaluation. By comparing activity in the kids' right temporo-parietal junction region to the results of false-belief tasks, they've been able to show the correlation between anatomical development and activity and the behavioral abilities of Theory of Mind, helping show the origins of the neural mechanism responsible for it.

Researchers worldwide have conducted numerous studies in recent decades on various aspects and levels of ToM development.

Simon Baron-Cohen, a leading autism researcher and professor at Cambridge University, found that by age nine, children could recognize when someone made a faux pas in speech, such as accidentally referring to a boy as a girl, or a waiter as a customer. By being able to read the intent of the speaker, they could recognize when a mistake was made. Interpreting meaning "in context" turns out to be a brain-skill that takes years to develop. Interestingly, at around age nine, girls' abilities at interpreting intent were slightly better than boys' abilities.

Take a few minutes to do the exercise on the next page. Without adequate training, a person with autism couldn't interpret someone's intent or do this exercise. One of my patients with Asperger syndrome, for instance, was eleven years old when he drew a series of cartoons about a fight he'd had with his mother. He told me he was sad about the fight, and I asked him to draw his face looking sad. With all seriousness, he drew himself, but with a grin from ear to ear. When I told him that was a happy face, he seemed genuinely astonished. "You mean the way our face looks is meant to tell someone else how we feel?" This boy had endured thousands of these interactions with many, many people over his eleven years of life, repeatedly astonished why grown-ups got mad at him and other children did not want him over for play-dates.

For the next several weeks, we drew various facial expressions and attached the correct emotions. My patient then looked in a mirror and moved his face to mimic the feeling he had inside. Although it never was intuitive, with practice he could quickly match his face to his feelings. He began to understand that his mom had been angry because she thought he was laughing at her. "I knew she was angry with me," he said, "but I didn't know why." Through her own intact Theory of Mind, she inferred disrespect. But when she learned that her son had not smiled with the intent to annoy her, she was no longer angry.

———————— Exercise ————————

THEORY OF MIND 101

Take a look at the six photos below and check the box next to the word you think best explains what you think the person is feeling in each one.

☐ Fear ☐ Surprise
☐ Joy ☐ Contempt
☐ Sadness ☐ Anger
☐ Disgust

☐ Fear ☐ Surprise
☐ Joy ☐ Contempt
☐ Sadness ☐ Anger
☐ Disgust

☐ Fear ☐ Surprise
☐ Joy ☐ Contempt
☐ Sadness ☐ Anger
☐ Disgust

☐ Fear ☐ Surprise
☐ Joy ☐ Contempt
☐ Sadness ☐ Anger
☐ Disgust

☐ Fear ☐ Surprise
☐ Joy ☐ Contempt
☐ Sadness ☐ Anger
☐ Disgust

☐ Fear ☐ Surprise
☐ Joy ☐ Contempt
☐ Sadness ☐ Anger
☐ Disgust

How do you know this? Well, you actually don't know for sure, but you've seen the expressions for these emotions on other people's faces innumerable times throughout your life. So, with no effort at all, your brain jumps in and makes a calculated guess. This guess will then influence how you behave with that other person, who then engages in a reciprocal social behavior. How well you read another person often dictates the quality of your social interaction.

SECRETS FROM OUR EVOLUTIONARY PAST

So where does Theory of Mind come from? And why have we evolved a distinct portion of brain matter explicitly for interpreting the thoughts of others? These are the questions that especially drive the work of evolutionary biologists and psychologists. The overarching theme that emerges from most of current research is that ToM became a factor that contributed to the survival potential of humans (and primates before us). Many groups have explored these questions, but one team from the University of Pennsylvania have theorized that the ability to attribute intention to others is what facilitated the formation of small social groups, a critical achievement in the evolution of human societies. In their study, published in the Proceedings of the National Academy of Sciences, authors Dorothy Cheney and Robert Seyfarth suggested that

> a subconscious, reflexive appreciation of others' intentions, emotions, and perspectives is at the roots of even the most complex forms of Theory of Mind and that these abilities may have evolved because natural selection has favored individuals that are motivated to empathize with others and attend to their social interactions. These skills are adaptive because they are essential to forming strong, enduring social bonds, which in turn enhance reproductive success.

And so it makes sense that ToM evolved as a critical brain tool allowing humans to communicate, which facilitated survival and procreation. Humans have survived because we are social animals, after all. Starting as a species competing with professional carnivores, we developed the ability to cooperate so effectively that we out-competed the very predators that used to hunt us.

▶ **I-M IMPACT: SAFETY IN 360**

Try this mental exercise. No matter what position your body is in, there is a large section of the world that you can't see: the areas to the sides and behind you. Without moving your head, check out how much of your surroundings you can see by moving your eyes as far as they'll go in any and all directions. Our field of view is about 190 degrees, or a little more than half a circle of 360 degrees.

Now imagine this, or actually try it: place someone back to back with you. These two sets of eyes cover the entire immediate world. The combined 190 degrees times two allows two people to scan their entire surroundings. Something moving in a bush, a possible predator, can be seen by the person behind you. And assuming that the person moves to avoid the predator, whether intentionally alerting you or not, you would also have the chance to avoid a predator that you hadn't even detected yourself. You literally have each other's backs!

When this coordination of people becomes planned, and not just a chance and coincidental occurrence, the home or social domain created can dramatically improve the survival potential of everyone in that group. Instead of one person trying to survive, two or more can share in that task. Our security systems have come a long way: from helping each other out in the bush or on the savannah to a world with radar detection systems and defense departments.

We're not just talking about safety, but survival. When we operate with these terms, we are directly impacting several key domains, those of the I-M Approach discussed in the introduction. We're considering our own bodily health and safety (our biological domain), our own psychology (Ic domain), our family and shelter (home domain), and our wider surroundings (social domain). Theory of Mind has a direct connection to human existence on every level of our everyday lives.

As we began to rely more on each other for survival, ToM had to develop so we could discern what another member of our tribe might be thinking or feeling. We may not have been consciously aware of wondering whether we could trust someone or not, or whether we should share our food with them now, perhaps anticipating a future return of the favor. We probably weren't consciously aware that being able to "read" another person's intentions actually helped us survive longer than people who couldn't. From an evolutionary point of view, our ancestors with this ability fared better than their relatives who did not. ToM became an advantage as important as the ability to stand on two legs, make tools, and form groups—skills that eventually turned the hunted into hunters. Indeed, it was the very foundation for human connection and communication. But how and why did this happen in our brains and our species? One has to look back even further in human history.

Ethiopia's Afar Rift is a bleak and forbidding place. Ancient volcanic activity has created meadows of magma, molten rock hardened into fields and ridges, the result of the very plates of the earth crashing up against each other billions of years ago. A boiling lake of lava still spills its fumes into the air, the earth around it bent and fissured into a bizarre landscape. Over the last several decades, this remote part of northern Ethiopia has been a literal hotbed of activity. For hidden in this land of active smoking volcanoes our oldest origins have been recently uncovered.

In 2009, a team of paleontologists discovered what is now thought to be the most ancient prehistoric fossils of an ancestral human. This fossil was found to be a pre–Homo sapiens female skeleton of a species they named *Ardipithecus ramidus*, taking the Afar words for *root* and *ground*. *Ardipithecus ramidus* lived 4.4 million years ago and may have emerged 6 million years ago as our earliest human relative. The team also nicknamed the skeleton itself Ardi, which denotes a ground-living ape near the root of the human family tree.

The fossil record that now starts with Ardi provides a visible history of pre-human physical development. In less than ten million years, a rather rapid pace when considering the hundreds of millions of preceding years, our bodies adapted to the challenges of the environment. The fossil trail reveals a gradual change in bone structure, from moving on all fours to walking upright. With this shift, thumbs began to emerge as we continued to free our hands for use while walking. The increasing size of the skull suggests that a larger brain had started to form the neo-cortex, the "new-brain." Certain parts of the brain were responsible for certain things. Of particular importance in human evolution is the frontal lobe, and in particular the prefrontal cortex in the front part of the skull, right behind the forehead.

Scientists have long hypothesized that a larger brain implied greater "intelligence": a belief bolstered by the appearance of ancient tools and some evidence of how they were being used perhaps as early as three million years ago. Throughout many parts of the world, archeologists have uncovered an array of variously chiseled flints used as spearheads or arrowheads. The ancient cave paintings in Lascaux, France, an amazing visual treasure depicting animal hunts and practices, have been dated to about 17,000 years ago. There is also a remarkable collection of 6,500-year-old skulls from a burial site elsewhere in France. Many of these skulls have burr holes drilled in them from a process called trepanning: making holes in a person's head to release so-called evil spirits. Tools, paintings, and other human relics provide many clues to the early human culture.

All combined, the evidence shows us that a few million years ago human beings began to live and flourish in groups. These more "modern" tools and drawings from tens of thousands of years ago reveal both cultures of cooperation and cultures of war. Images of compassion are coupled with images of brutality. Why did humans evolve these particular behaviors and not others?

Why did these two poles of behavior, cooperation and competition, influence so heavily the development of society, even as we know it today?

Tracing the physical evolution of our human ancestors is painstaking work. But mapping the evolution of behaviors is even more challenging. And trying to figure out the evolution of Theory of Mind? That had been confined only to speculation until quite recently. In just the last decade, advances in biochemistry and neuroimaging have let us see and even measure evolutionary pathways in the brain. These pathways have been found in the form of brain chemicals called *neurohormones,* which power the machinery running our brains and bodies.

A ROAD MAP BACK IN TIME:
OXYTOCIN AND VASOPRESSIN

In 1906, Sir Henry Dale, an English pharmacologist and physiologist, first discovered a nine-amino-acid central nervous system neuropeptide, when he found that extracts from part of the human brain called the posterior pituitary gland could contract the uterus of a pregnant cat. Dale coined the name *oxytocin* from the Greek words meaning *swift birth.*

Since its discovery, scientists have learned a great deal more about this neurohormone, which influences a range of prosocial behaviors and biological responses in both animals and humans. Oxytocin is now widely recognized as the "trust hormone" or "cuddle hormone" due to its release in mothers nurturing infants. It influences the way a mother and child interact, the way people bond with each other, and the way they communicate with each other. It is widely considered the neurohormone of trust and attachment, without which humanity could never have survived. As we've seen, social bonding is essential to species survival since it favors reproduction and protects against predators and environmental changes, as well as shaping brain development.

Oxytocin is therefore a key building block of ToM. But it's not the only one. Another neurohormone, vasopressin, also plays a leading role because of its influence on a range of behaviors and biological responses, especially with regard to aggression.

▶ **NONOPEPTIDES? YES, YES!**

The cells of plants and animals are like tiny cities or castles encased within a wall with many doors and windows. Each is surrounded by its bastions with several drawbridges that can be raised or lowered to insulate from or connect to the outside world. Like any city, a cell needs energy to run. It produces garbage that must be disposed of, buildings and roads that need to be built and maintained, and ways to get and distribute food. All of these duties are handled by collections of molecules called proteins (or enzymes). Most proteins are made up of a string of smaller chemicals called amino acids. These strings then twist and turn into various shapes that allow for various functions. For example, insulin is made up of fifty-one amino acids folded and twisted to make a perfect carriage for glucose, the source of energy to run most of the rest of the enzyme machines in the cell. There is compelling evidence that the insulin molecule itself has been around in some form for a billion years.

What is really amazing is that the two neurohormones involved in our complex human behaviors, oxytocin and vasopressin, are made up of only nine amino acids each. Just nine. As such, they have the scientific name *nonopeptides*, proteins (*peptides*) made up of nine (*nono*) amino acids that fit together like puzzle pieces. These two nonopeptides emerge early in the growing fetus: vasopressin at eleven weeks, oxytocin at fourteen. As we know, oxytocin is involved in trust and attachment to each other, like mothers and their babies, or lovers, or members of the same tribe. Meanwhile, vasopressin is involved in aggression and war, and is found in the victims of bullying. Not only that, it's an antidiuretic hormone, involved in regulating urine. Combine these two responsibilities, aggression and urination, and you get a whole new meaning to the phrase *pissed off!*

In fact, all animals with backbones, or vertebrates, have some form of oxytocin- and vasopressin-like proteins that have evolved from another form of the substance, vasotocin. Several invertebrate species, those without backbones, also have analogous proteins: creatures like clams and oysters, ringworms, roundworms, ants, spiders, and shrimp. The fact that these creatures have those similar proteins suggests that oxytocin and vasopressin are related across the entire animal kingdom.

The presence of these protein cousins suggests that ancient, pre-hominid creatures were already secreting chemicals that have travelled as our companions through evolution as fundamental neural compounds over millions of years. Vasotocin itself may have emerged even earlier in animals 700 million years ago, the precursor perhaps even to oxytocin itself. This would make sense in an environment where every living creature was out for itself, constantly competing for limited resources such as food, shelter, and the ability to reproduce. Aggression was the only way to survive, as it still is today for predatory animals in the wild.

But somewhere in our evolution, our ancient ancestors stumbled upon a remarkable survival strategy. Rather than try to fend alone, some of them, sometime, somewhere, must have survived better together, while relatives who didn't band together in these small protective groups didn't fare as well—some perhaps falling prey themselves to the growing band of pre-human beings. The progression of human life from isolated individuals to social groups had begun. Aggression itself, aided by vasopressin, now had a competitor: cooperation, aided by oxytocin. This evolutionary story may explain the two driving forces so intimately connected with human evolution and ToM: our aggressive, competitive side, balanced by our compassionate, trusting side.

Watch Out for Vasopressin

Also an antidiuretic hormone, vasopressin is a critical neurohormone that the brain calls in to regulate wide-ranging body functions: for example, blood volume, blood pressure, and level of salts in the blood. Think of *vaso-* as blood vessels, and *pressin-* as pressing or squeezing those vessels. Where does vasopressin come into the picture of human bonding? It regulates important aspects of social behavior, specifically aggression of the protective kind.

In this case, vasopressin bonds one person to the other—but around the joy and relief one experiences when defeating an enemy. Scientists believe that vasopressin may make it easier for individuals to become aggressive by influencing both the limbic system and the prefrontal cortex. By suppressing empathy toward an out-group, vasopressin works to place the limbic system more in charge of the brain. A limbic brain is an ancient protective, impulsive, and aggressive brain, one that harnesses the plan-building capacity of the prefrontal cortex and bends it to its will. We have the ability to become extremely limbic, but in order to really hurt someone else we have to shut down empathy: we have to shut down Theory of Mind.

Imagine having an argument, especially one with someone you really care about. Could you or the other person say nasty and hurtful things to each other? Has it ever happened to you? If you're like most people, you'd have to admit yes, even though later you would say you didn't mean it. Whenever you say something mean to someone in an argument, it's coming from a limbic, emotional place—you've temporarily shut down your ToM and empathy. Empathy is designed to decrease the chance of hurting someone, and being hurt. So how does this override happen? Vasopressin.

We elicit empathy to get someone else to bond to us and help us in a time of need. But when researchers at Hebrew University in Jerusalem gave vasopressin to male study volunteers, it became harder for the subjects to identify negative emotions like fear and anger. The vasopressin didn't change how the subjects recognized positive emotions like interest, enthusiasm, laughter, empathy, and curiosity. Instead, the vasopressin only made it easier to override *negative* emotions, giving the green light to exclusion and alienation.

So as vasopressin serves to exclude for protective reasons, when it comes to the hormonal recipe for true bonding, vasopressin cannot work without its mate, oxytocin.

Make Way for Oxytocin

What is frequently seen as mother's love is in fact driven by the neurohormone oxytocin, which is widely recognized as the major brain chemical involved in creating and rearing offspring. The unique actions of oxytocin include starting the birth process, breastfeeding, and maternal and caring behavior. In mammals, it sends a signal to the uterus that it's time to contract and deliver a baby. Maybe you've heard of Pitocin, the medication given to women to jumpstart labor: it's a synthetic form of oxytocin. Oxytocin begins the milk let-down, the process by which mammals release breast milk to feed their newborns. Hundreds of studies support the theory that it's a critical component for orchestrating reproductive behaviors and the prosocial in-group supportive behaviors that make a person want to remain part of a club. It's involved in the reproductive behaviors in some non-mammals as well, including egg-laying species like chickens and snakes. Believe it or not, traces of oxytocin-like chemicals can even be found in worms. Animals with plenty of this hormone tend to their young, nurturing them, protecting them from predators. In humans, this can go on for decades.

Oxytocin is also involved in the actual growth of the brain, and maintaining its blood supply. Neurobiologist Dr. C. S. Carter suggests that oxytocin may have been necessary for the evolution and development of the human brain as we know it today. It facilitated the attachment between a parent and child, allowing for

> the extended periods of nurture necessary for the emergence of human intellectual development. In general, oxytocin acts to allow the high levels of social sensitivity and attunement necessary for human sociality and for rearing a human child. Under optimal conditions oxytocin may create an emotional sense of safety.

Without this social sensitivity, human relationships could not have evolved, nor families, nor societies or cultures. We as a species would not exist, and would never have existed, without oxytocin. Theory of Mind, of course, could never have evolved either.

MATCHING NEURONS

But hormones are not working alone in the mechanism behind Theory of Mind. Have you ever felt sad when watching a sad movie? Or happy when watching a romantic comedy? Human beings have a remarkable ability to mirror what another person is feeling. We have special brain cells responsible for this ability. Not surprisingly, they're called *mirror neurons*.

Mirror neurons were first discovered in 1996 when the brain waves from 532 neurons in two macaque monkeys were intensely examined by researchers at the University di Parma in Italy. When one monkey watched the other monkey grasp a peanut, his brain cells activated as if he were grasping it himself. These neurons are in the *premotor cortex,* the brain part that prepares the body for action. Initially, mirror neurons were thought to be involved in motion only. But we now know they are also involved in emotions.

How often do we see a young child copy what a parent is doing? When a toddler sees her father smiling and humming while he's washing the dishes, she comes to the sink to join in. And when baby brother begins to cry, that same toddler begins to cry too, apparently in sympathy, or perhaps thinking something must be scaring her brother.

When several people in a crowd begin to fight, say in a soccer stadium, the fighting soon spreads and becomes a mob brawl, especially if fueled by alcohol. Everyone in the crowd goes crazy. But this mirroring can work the other way, too. In 1989, the congregation of St. Nikolai's Lutheran Church in Leipzig, then East Germany, gathered outside the church with candles and quietly chanted, "We are the people." This hushed, peaceful demonstration projected the desire for a unified Germany. Every Monday evening, people gathered in other parts of the city and then in other town squares all over East Germany in what became known as the Monday Revolution. This peaceful demonstration helped bring down the Berlin Wall. More recently, we saw similar "mirroring" in the so-called Arab Spring uprising.

Some scientists believe that the interplay between ToM and mirror neurons is the foundation of culture. We imitate each other's behavior as a way of fitting in, of maintaining membership. From a survival point of view, if I see another human from my group climb a tree and pick a mango, I may want to do the same thing. Mirror neurons have evolved as a way to consider doing just that. But they don't just prompt imitations. They actually become more active when we observe movements that have social significance. When I observe someone behaving in a social situation, I'm assessing whether or not I want to do the same thing. As each of us uses mirror neurons for this purpose, each of us can have profound influence on the social behavior of another person.

Of course, we know this intuitively, but understanding the brain science behind this intuition gives us the chance to transform it into a technique.

Mirror neurons activate even if the observer knows that climbing the tree will not yield any mangos. Instead, we can interpret the intention of other people and their desire to get a mango, even if we know there are no mangoes to be had. This ability to infer is also a function of ToM: understanding the viewpoint and intent of another. Understanding intent is information that can help us respond more productively and successfully. We use the same language, and have facial expressions that communicate our inner world of thought and feeling. Mirror neurons are part and parcel of our evolution. We can use them to project peace or to stir up trouble.

▶ **ATTRIBUTING INTENTION**

Every day, completely unconsciously, we attribute intention using our built-in Theory of Mind. We don't even need words to do this, which hints at the evolution of this trait well before language evolved among pre-humans. Here are a few common situations that illustrate this skill. Do you recognize your own abilities at this?

1. You and a young woman walk up to a coffee stand at the same moment. You are clearly in a hurry. She motions with her eyes and smile for you to order first. You didn't have to say a word; she knew your intent and you knew hers, so you recognize it and tell her "thank you."

2. You're getting on the bus or train and looking for a seat. As you go down the aisle, you see row after row of lone riders who've put their belongings in the aisle seat. You come upon a fellow who looks reasonable and catch his eye. Without saying a word, he removes his bag so you can sit down. You say thanks,

because he used ToM to attribute intention. As simple as this seems, you oftentimes actually have to stop and ask someone if the seat is taken. The person then may grudgingly clear the seat, perhaps avoiding eye contact, fixated on a smartphone, and choosing not to use ToM in that moment. You immediately feel uneasy around this person, which tells you how antisocial it feels when we don't apply ToM. In fact, people who don't clear the seat may actually *be* using ToM, but are choosing to send the message that they don't care about you (or anyone else). ToM can be used to make other people feel bad as well as good.

3. You're driving around the parking lot looking for a spot. You see someone's taillights come on, and you stop and wait. When the person pulls out, another car from the other side nabs the spot. You feel angry because that driver either took the spot knowing your intention, or he took the spot because he *didn't* know your intention. Maybe your blinker wasn't on? Maybe the person has dementia or other neurological impairment? Maybe the person was just selfish? In this scenario, you felt that your intention was clear, but another didn't attribute it. Witness the frustration between people when ToM is interrupted.

THEORY OF MIND IN THE DEVELOPING BRAIN

As we've seen, the development of ToM in the brain has paralleled our evolution as a species. It also parallels actual human physical development from crawling to standing, walking, and the ability to wander away. For instance, by around eight months old, most babies are starting to crawl, and at the same time are starting to experience stranger anxiety. It would make evolutionary sense that an unfamiliar face is a potentially dangerous person, even to an adult. But the baby, too young to rationalize, begins to yell and squirm, trying to get away from the stranger. If the stranger really is dangerous, help will come. If the stranger is not dangerous, then no harm is done. But if that baby happens to be *your* baby, and the stranger happens to be *your* mom or dad, or perhaps worse, your *in-laws* on a visit to the baby, it can be quite embarrassing that little Jimmy won't let himself be held by Grandma. Fortunately, with time, Jimmy will learn that Grandma's is a kind face; she is no longer a stranger to fear.

When a child begins to walk, with the potential to wander farther from home, the requirements for more sophisticated brain interpretation increase. A three-year-old reacts differently from a five-year-old in assessing a stranger. From an evolutionary point of view, it makes sense to move to a more sophisticated and selective approach to a stranger. First, the child may find herself too far away from the caregiver for screaming to do much good. Second, because help is unlikely to arrive on time, it would make more sense to assess the stranger quietly, without drawing too much attention to herself. By assessing the possible intention of that stranger, she could decide whether to get home as soon as possible, or perhaps to find another person for shelter and safety.

Human beings are really good at comparing sets of information, a primitive survival technique that has served us well and has helped allow us to "read" each other's intentions even when first meeting. With a word, a look, a tone of voice, a shrug of the shoulder, a wave of a hand, or a shake of a fist, our brains instantly attribute intention to that other person, and we theorize about that person's thoughts and feelings. In fact, these first impressions are formed extremely quickly, within the first 39 milliseconds, less than the blink of an eye. This ability involves the direct application of ToM. When a child ventures away from the confines of a familiar group, this ability to compare information rapidly and effectively can become critical to survival.

Yet an unforeseen consequence accompanies our ability to appreciate what another person is thinking or feeling: that other person was wondering about *your* thoughts and feelings as well. ToM demands that you convince the other person that you are indeed a person to be trusted. And paradoxically, that very same trust has led to one of the more pernicious human behaviors, one that even my little Sophie may have been doing when she covered her eyes and ate that lollipop, one that human beings are really, really good at with sometimes devastating results. Human beings have developed the ability to distort Theory of Mind to their benefit in the form of a lie, a phenomenon you're about to explore in the next chapter.

2

Untruth

THE ART OF LYING

Three things cannot be long hidden:
the sun, the moon, and the truth.
—**Buddha**

O, what a tangled web we weave,
when first we practice to deceive.
—**Sir Walter Scott, *Marmion***

"Have you weighed yourself since we got back?" my wife asked.

"No," I lied.

"Yes, you have. You're lying." She was right. I had been on a diet before heading off on vacation. I'd intended to at least maintain my weight, but I had put back three pounds. So I lied. And my best friend since 1978 knew it.

"I've never lied to you," I lied again.

A gentle smile emerged, paired with a barely creased forehead that slightly tugged up her eyebrows. Combined with the casual tilt of her head, this picture was indeed worth a thousand words, distilled down to two: "Oh, yeah?" And we both laughed.

Why did I lie? How did my wife know I was lying? How did I then know, based on her expression, that she knew I was lying?

That's what the next level of Theory of Mind is all about: two people inferring what the other is thinking and feeling and deciding if they can trust each other. Without trust, one or the other is probably going to walk away. Only if trust is given will the interaction potentially turn into an exchange: be it in commerce, employment, a date with a potential mate, a vote for a candidate, all the way to a peace treaty between countries.

In this instance with my wife, we were both using ToM fluidly at the same time, resulting in a remarkably clear yet nuanced communication.

But why on earth did I have an urge to lie at all?

Being untruthful about the three pounds I'd gained wasn't hurting my wife, although a more serious lie could have had an influence on our relationship. As we both laughed, I admitted I had weighed myself, felt ashamed and embarrassed, and was mad at myself for not being able to maintain those first few enthusiastic days of dieting and succumbing to culinary temptation. This "white lie" was told so that I would remain esteemed in my wife's eyes, and she knew that. So instead of becoming angry, my wife congratulated me on only putting on three, and she encouraged me to keep up my quest to lose weight.

As you now know, we human beings have developed ToM to assess what other people think or feel—about us, and in general. The root of this interest has many factors, but two key motives stand out: value and influence.

THEORY OF MIND AND VALUE

We use ToM to assess if we are seen as valuable through the eyes of others. When you're viewed as valuable, you feel valued and can relax because you get to stay within the protective group: a relationship, a company, a family, and so on. You can trust a bit more, and that trust is bolstered by the release of oxytocin. But if you think you've lost your value, or that value is in any way diminished, your anxiety increases as you worry you may be kicked out of that protective group and have to fend for yourself, a vulnerable mammal in a world of vasopressin-driven aggressors.

Imagine for a moment what it feels like if someone accuses you of doing something you didn't do. Doubt is cast upon you, forcing your perceived value to go down. When your value is diminished, your anxiety skyrockets because you are trusted less. Trust is the currency we need in personal relationships. When you are not trusted, you feel less safe and protected by the social support and protection provided by a group. In the early days of our evolving species we joined together in tribes to survive. Banishment from the tribe meant certain death. Today the influence of group psychology has changed little. In many tribes and religious groups, even within the borders of Western nations, people would choose being accepted by others over having individual rights and freedoms. This is how intrinsically important it is for us to be valued and the only way we know we're valued is through the eyes of others.

THEORY OF MIND AND INFLUENCE

The other critical reason we're interested in what other people think or feel is to assess how we can influence those thoughts and feelings, and thereby potentially guide others' perception of us and actions toward us. Most of the time we try to influence people to do things for our benefit by convincing them that their actions will actually benefit *them* as well, increasing their overall value and survival potential. While this might sound premeditated, in reality it's completely unconscious. We have developed these practices for millennia to survive, just like learning to walk and talk.

As a result of our deep-seated need to be valued and to influence others' assessments, we humans have also come to be expert at exploiting ToM, which takes the form of subtle manipulation or, if we're being direct, lying.

Fibs, Fabrications, and Fictions

What is lying, anyway? It means conveying information that is meant to deceive or mislead. Lies are told for a variety of reasons, not always malicious, and quite often with the best of intentions. We have so many different words for these dishonesties: white lies, fibs, falsehoods, fabrications, tall tales, cock-and-bull stories, fictions, whoppers, stretching the truth, gilding, spinning, and many more. Few of us would call ourselves a liar, and to call someone else a liar is a particularly nasty insult. But the fact remains that most of us are consistently "dishonest" on some level. According to a number of studies on lying behaviors, measured in self-assessment surveys, the vast majority of us lie at least once or twice a day. Men self-report lying more than women do. Most people tell few lies—an honest majority—while a few people tell the most lies—prolific liars. Most people freely admit they lie to keep the wheels of social interaction lubricated and to avoid hurting feelings. But all deception has something in common: we don't lie just to lie. When we do it, we have a reason—we have something to protect, especially our value in the eyes of others, and we want to influence perception, creating a favorable outcome for ourselves.

How We Lie: White and Strategic

You've no doubt heard the term *white lie*. It's the one we tell to maintain our social status or to avoid hurting someone's feelings. White lies help us to preserve an image of ourselves, like my lie to my wife about my weight. We generally consider the white lie to be benign, even innocent, not meant to harm but to protect, or to get away with something minor. It shouldn't come as a surprise that along with their developing ability at ToM, young children have usually mastered the white lie by a mere three years old, and it's mainly because they observed their own family members doing it. Research also shows that the more children are lied to, the more they too will lie.

I witnessed a real doozy of a white lie in my own household a number of years ago. One early morning I heard yelling from the kitchen and went downstairs to find my three-year-old son had sneaked into the walk-in pantry and climbed onto the counter. Chocolate-covered cream-filled cookies were scattered on the floor, each pulled apart into its two halves. My son was screaming in fright, harassed by a dive-bombing bee attracted to the chocolate that dappled my child's face. The bee buzzed around the chocolate streaks that were concentrated around my boy's mouth, also flitting to his cheeks, forehead, hands, and pajamas where the chocolate had migrated in a steady trail.

After shooing the bee away, I gently lifted my son off the ledge on which he had been trapped, and asked if he had been licking the chocolate off the coated cookies.

"Oh no, Dad," he said to me sincerely. "Not me. I would never do that!"

His face was covered in chocolate. Perhaps because he was so young he still could not appreciate that I *saw* his face covered in chocolate. The door to the pantry cabinet stood open, and I could see that a box of chocolate-covered cookies had been quietly opened. But he lied because he must have had some moral sense (or just fear of punishment?) to know that I wouldn't approve of his eating cookies early in the morning without permission, and wanted me to see him a certain way: as a good and obedient boy, a person of value. He knew he wasn't meant to eat the cookies without permission, or he wouldn't have sneaked into the kitchen to begin with. But the urge was overwhelming, and he took the calculated risk of being caught, never anticipating the hungry bee.

Children begin to lie in parallel with the development of Theory of Mind, usually around the age of three. Once they develop the ability to appreciate another person's point of view, they begin to recognize that their value is influenced by how that other person views them. As parents and grown-ups, we assist in this process. A kid who is praised is likely to repeat the praised behavior later. A child who is scolded is less likely to repeat that behavior (we hope). But at some point, the same child who has performed a "bad" behavior may try to avoid the unpleasant experience of a scolding by trying to mislead the other person. ("Malik pulled my hair!" wails little Aliyah, while Malik swears he didn't do it.) With the lie, he can both avoid a scolding and maintain his "good-kid" Ic domain—until of course, he gets caught.

▶ COMPLIMENTS, FLATTERY, AND POLISHING APPLES

In Japan, people call someone who is obviously using flattery to get ahead a *goma-suri*, an apple polisher. Here we call them sycophants, and when we're disgusted by their behavior, asskissers, because it seems like everyone else can see their lies except perhaps the target of them. Yet, social groups somehow are able to draw a line in the sand when they see a little bit of flattery taken to extremes. We understand why people behave this way: they're obviously trying to get ahead, but when you try too hard to make yourself trustworthy, people begin to mistrust you. The least liked and least trusted person in the office is inevitably the apple polisher.

But we all have a little bit of excess flattery in us. Because our ToM is active, we're always trying to smooth the way, grease the social wheels, build trust. How often do you compliment someone on his or her ugly sweater, bad haircut, or hideous new curtains, when inside you're thinking "Dear lord"? Do you think of this as a lie? If you're like most people, you probably don't. We say things we don't necessarily believe to make others feel good. And we try to say these things very convincingly. When we succeed, we help others feel good; they feel relaxed, and we feel relaxed as we both accept each other, despite our untruthfulness.

Scientists have long been fascinated with lying in young children, because it reveals a great deal about the evolution of human behaviors in societies—rooted in part by Theory of Mind. One of the classic assessments of lying is called the peeking test. A child is brought into a room and sits facing away from the examiner. The two play a guessing game: the examiner produces a toy, like a duck, and plays the sound of a duck quacking. By the sound, the child is asked to guess what the toy is. For example, the child may identify a duck by its quacking, a lion by its roaring, or a frog by its croaking.

But then the child hears a piece of music, which gives no clue about the next toy. At that point the examiner gets a phone call or has some other reason to leave the room. She covers the toy with a cloth and tells the child not to turn around and peek; they'll continue the game when she gets back. The examiner then leaves for a few minutes, and when she returns, she asks the child to be honest and not lie: did the child peek at the hidden toy?

What do you think? Did they all peek, even when asked not to? It turns out that almost 90 percent of children under three do in fact peek.

But it's not because they are "bad" kids. It's likely for two perfectly logical reasons. First, the child's ToM and the interest in what other people think—combined with the desire for praise in knowing the right answer—is a strong temptation. Second, consider the fact that the impulsive area of the three-year-old brain dominates the thoughtful part. Impulse control studies in children consistently show similar results. For instance, another peeking test done at the University of Southern California among youngsters eight to sixteen showed that the older kids were significantly less likely to lie than the younger ones.

But before the honesty kicks in, there sure are some sophisticated mental gymnastics going on in those tiny brains. Recently, researchers from the University of Ontario used the peeking test to study sixty-five toddlers, two and three years old. What they discovered was that the two-year-olds were more likely to confess to peeking at the toy. But by the age of three, more peekers denied the peeking and lied. This could be seen as a distressing insight into who we are as human beings, as revealed through our early manipulations with the truth. But the flip side has to do with Theory of Mind. Children who know that another person may see them as "less-than" because they cheated and peeked are more likely to attempt to preserve their value through the eyes of others by lying and trying to maintain their image as being trustworthy. In fact, the ability to anticipate the future is a good predictor of which children are more likely to lie: children with more robust executive functioning were more likely to lie. Thankfully, for most children this is a normal developmental phase, as it was for my three-year-old son, who is now a young adult with terrific social skills, and who is, I believe, quite honest.

We have long carried the habit of white lies, even referred to as benevolent lies, well into adulthood, and even into our professional lives. In many professions, business leaders have long been taught to believe that certain types of lying are actually good, and considered even better than the truth. The medical profession for one, a field where trust has always been deemed of the utmost importance, has not been always been the most truthful. As a paternalistic establishment, medicine long wielded an undisputable authority about what was best for patients. In the last decades, this dogma has changed dramatically, especially when it comes to how honest doctors need to be. Today, we have a patient agreement called informed consent to assure that patients know what medical options are available to treat their condition, the potential risks and benefits of each, and the risks and benefits of no treatment at all.

Yet, when I was being trained as a young doctor, these reforms hadn't yet come about. We doctors routinely thought we knew better. I recall the case of a woman in her mid-thirties who had presented to the medical team myriad symptoms, none of which made any real physical sense, including a scattered paralysis that seemed to have no neurological basis. Some muscles worked when they shouldn't; others didn't when they should. She seemed to have no ability to sense pressure or feel anything on her skin at all. There were no rashes and no apparent traumas. Multiple sclerosis, a condition where a person can get these sorts of random malfunctions, had been ruled out, as well as even the most rare causes of such a bizarre presentation. She hadn't responded to any traditional medication, and she'd tried various herbal remedies and acupuncture before she came to the hospital.

So I prescribed Obecalp, two pills three times a day. My psychiatry supervisor told the patient that the medication might not work, but that in her experience the vast majority of patients, within even a few days, would get some sensation and feeling back in their limbs. They would begin to move the same muscles that had been dormant just a few days before. The psychiatrist warned her that after this the progress was slow but incremental, and she shouldn't be dismayed if it took longer for her to "get back on her feet" than she hoped for.

And then we watched. After just two days of Obecalp, the woman's sensation began to return, along with some small muscle movement. My supervisor commented on how unusually fast this recovery was, and our patient grinned. Within a few days of treatment, two pills three times a day, our patient was walking down the hallway, enjoying the company of a physical therapist. The Obecalp worked for our patient, but it's no longer given the way it was in those years. What's Obecalp? Spell it backwards: it's "placebo."

To this day I am amazed, if not sometimes disturbed, by this case. While it's not illegal to use placebos, many view their use as unethical and it has become a subject of some debate. But it's worth noting that placebos have been in use for centuries, and they do have a record of effectiveness, which is now, ironically, being studied.

A placebo, which means *I shall please* in Latin, is indeed a dummy treatment; a lie, if you will. But is receiving a placebo the same as being lied to? Concretely, the answer is yes: I tell my patients they're receiving one thing, but in reality they're taking something different. And yet there's compelling evidence that some people respond as well to the placebo effect as to "active" medications. So could giving a placebo actually be morally acceptable when a caregiver has "virtue-based ethical orientation"— is doing it with the best interest of the patient at heart?

The placebo effect depends on the expectations of the patient. Those expectations involve ToM: one person, the doctor or care provider, is sharing a viewpoint with the patient, who develops expectations and beliefs based on specific wishes and desires, pain relief, for instance. No surprise, but the prefrontal cortex is involved in this process, along with other brain areas like the amygdala, the site of emotional memory. The placebo effect, however, still remains a medical mystery.

So white lies come in many sizes and shapes, from lying about stealing cookies to treating patients with sugar pills. Nobody may get hurt, and nobody is out to make a profit from it, but dishonesty on any level is not easily forgotten. When we hold someone to higher standards—such as in medicine, journalism, or government—such untruthful bargains erode trust, which often takes great effort to rebuild.

On an everyday level, white lies are often used to soften a blow or, ironically, to show respect. I was recently in an Uber car with a driver who was wearing a hat pulled down over his ears. To navigate traffic, he had his cell phone in front of him flashing various route options. I happened to be chatting with him about Theory of Mind, and he told me how he surreptitiously wore a Bluetooth earpiece, which was hidden by his hat. He explained that while the law dictated he couldn't use the device, he didn't want his passengers disturbed by the grating voice of the GPS telling him which way to go. He felt that would be disrespectful. So he was essentially lying, and breaking the law, in order to protect his passengers.

This story illustrates that lying isn't always so easy to decipher. A lie may be used to deceive one person with the purpose of benefiting someone else.

Now think of some examples in your life, and try to determine when you think a lie was justified and when the truth might have been more helpful.

 Exercise

ME, TELL A LIE?

Yes—you, me, and, everyone we know. It's our Theory of Mind at work keeping others feeling good about themselves and thus valued. It's about your feeling good through the eyes of others and working to keep us all feeling respected and valued by each other. You can gain a better understanding of how your own ToM works by seeing where you are more apt to lie in your life. From this list, circle the areas of your life you have lied about—and lie about the most, and then ask yourself why.

Height	Health	Income
Education	Age	Background
Weight	Experience	Skills

And to whom have you lied? Circle all that apply:

Parents   Law Enforcement   Siblings

                         Boss
        Customers   Strangers
                         Kids

Colleagues   Spouse   Friends

I-M Impact: What you probably discovered in most of these cases is that you were untruthful because you didn't want to lose value in the eyes of the person you lied to, or you wanted to boost your value in someone else's eyes. Remember, it's for these same reasons that others lie to us. When we understand that we're all doing the best we can in any given moment (the I-Maximum Approach), we can forgive ourselves and others for wanting and needing to be valued. Maybe we can even start to lie a little less.

Pathological Lying

You often hear people casually say, "Oh, she's a pathological liar," and in some cases they might be right. Someone who is constantly spouting untruths or spinning dazzling tales for no apparent gain is someone who suffers from what we in psychiatry also refer to as *pseudologia fantastica* or *mythomania*.

In general, scientists know little about why people become pathological liars. A 2008 study by Canadian researchers on repeat juvenile offenders found that one in a thousand exhibited pathological lying behaviors. That's not a tiny number, and it certainly could be an underestimate. In fact, many of the subjects may have been lying when they said that they didn't lie. A pattern that's been observed in research among pathological liars is the tendency to invent grandiose tales to inflate their image. Perhaps their lives weren't very interesting and they wanted to impress. In this case, they too were using ToM to enhance their perceived value, but they couldn't understand that without trust, there is no value. It is this desire for internal gain, as opposed to external gain, that separates pathological lying from psychopathic lying—a sinister cousin solely intended to deceive others for the material gain of the liar.

You may have heard of a condition called Munchausen syndrome, and its cousin, Munchausen by proxy. Patients with this condition lie about their medical symptoms, sometimes incurring multiple surgical procedures, baffling their medical team as one symptom leads to the next. I was once called to consult on a young child who had undergone several surgeries for vomiting of unknown origin. His mother was delightful and charming, an ideal parent who spent lots of time in the hospital with her child. The mother was the darling of the nurses, who tended to her with enormous compassion. After all, she had a very sick child.

But in reality, there was nothing wrong with her child. One day when a nurse entered the patient's room unexpectedly, she found the mother making the child drink Ipecac to induce vomiting. This was Munchausen by proxy. In order to feel valuable, the mother was lying about the sickness of her child. The diagnosis was made, and I was able to talk with the mother. She revealed a history of being abused as a child herself, and she wanted her own child to be in the protection of doctors and nurses. This mom had used ToM to make the medical team feel special, needed, and invested in finding the cause of her child's chronic vomiting.

By contrast, there are some individuals who are incapable of lying. People with Asperger syndrome, who are already challenged with a lack of Theory of Mind, are virtually incapable of lying. They cannot conceive of any gain in lying to express respect for someone else, and they expect everyone else to tell the truth as well, ruthless or not. For this reason, those on the autistic spectrum are unfortunately very gullible, as they trust in the absolute truth of what other people say.

Strategic Lying to Influence

Not all lies are "white." Some people tell a much darker type of lie, the *strategic lie*, the kind told when a person or group intentionally tries to deceive for personal gain. One of the biggest strategic lies in recent history was revealed to the public in 2008, in the form of one magical investor named Bernie Madoff. For more than thirty years, Madoff built a legitimate financial trading company as well as an exclusive investment fund for the ultra-wealthy. For those investors, the "fund" seemed impermeable to the cyclical downs of the market, and a person needed the right connection to even get into it. But with the collapse of the economy in 2008, the Madoff fund was revealed as the Ponzi scheme it always was. The total loss of the fund was reported at $65 billion. People lost millions, some their life savings, and at the age of seventy-one, Madoff was sentenced to 150 years in prison.

Tellingly, even though Madoff had commanded the respect of Wall Street for decades, sentencing judge Denny Chin emphasized that not one person—not a friend, family member, or other supporter—had submitted any letter on behalf of Madoff's character or contributions to the community. A lie on this scale, with the damage it caused to so many people and organizations, highlights the reason we don't like liars and we don't like lying. It completely distorts the whole notion of ToM as our invisible liaison to trust.

Society has given a name to people who set out to strategically lie to us. They're called con artists, *con* being an abbreviation for *confidence*. The skilled con artist uses Theory of Mind with great cunning, instilling confidence and trust in others, and then exploiting this trust to steal something, usually money. Con artists are professional liars who have completely manipulated human behavior to their gain. They know they're lying, and they know why they're lying. Not surprisingly, they are known to be some of the most charming people in the world, as was Bernie Madoff, author James Frey, cyclist Lance Armstrong, President Richard Nixon (and probably most politicians to a degree), to name a few in the public eye.

But the underlying motive for strategic lying is often more than money: it's to gain or maintain influence and power. Although Madoff had legitimately earned respect through his other financial dealings, it was clearly not enough for his ego (he surely didn't need the money). Some of the most frequently heard strategic lies can be found plentifully on the internet and are designed to entrap another person into giving money or divulging secrets. No doubt you've seen them, hopefully you laughed at them, and quickly deleted them: "Dear so-and-so, please help me. I am doing overseas mission work and all my money has been stolen. Can you send me some cash? I will pay you back when I get home." Or "Congratulations, you have won the Irish Lottery. Your check is waiting. Please send us your bank account information so we can deposit your winnings." Or one of my current favorites, "I am in Portugal and need a kidney transplant. The medical cost is so much less here in Portugal, but my time is running out. Please send me some money so I can get my kidney."

The trouble is, enough of these ruses are successful that they just keep getting more creative. According to a U.S. government report on internet crime, Americans lost $198.4 million to Internet fraud in 2006, with an average loss of $5,100 per victim. Today the FBI even has a designated Internet Crime Complaint Center.

Modern society is filled with the lesser tales of malicious deceptions. Indeed, our desire for success can be a double-edged sword, one that can be readily exploited by people who specialize in tapping into our desire to be valued and valuable. That's the message of most modern marketing and advertising—if you use our product, you will be perceived as more valuable. Indeed, our need to be valued by others makes us ripe fruit to be deceived. Not surprisingly, most of the world's largest advertising agencies hire not just psychologists but also anthropologists to shed light on how the human mind ticks.

Buy this deodorant and you'll be more accepted. Wear these clothes and you'll be hot. Join this club and you'll be special. Use this credit card and everyone will think you're rich. One recent radio ad declares in velvet tones, "What you drive says who you are." I drive an old beat-up Lincoln. What does that say about who I am? Personally, I don't think it says much. But another person, one on the hunt for more perceived value from others, may go and buy a car based on who they want others to think they are. In fact, there's perhaps no better evidence of how our ToM is constantly churning than the success of marketing products to enhance our image. We sure do care about what others think of us, and we spend millions trying to influence others.

But I would argue that consumerism, and strategic lying and deception, do not add up to lasting influence. If you want to influence people in a meaningful way, you need to think about building trust, a trust based on honesty and integrity—the bedrock of respect and trust—which leads to meaningful value in all relationships and groups. But how? Especially with all the obstacles you might be facing in your life? The answer is both in Theory of Mind and the I-M Approach.

THE I-MAXIMUM FACTOR IN LYING

"Be kind. Everyone you meet is fighting a hard battle." That popular expression has been attributed to Plato, though other sources name the Scottish theologian John Watson. Either way, the expression is apt for the vast truth it holds. Life presents struggles at various stages and in sundry ways, and if you're human you're not immune. This is because all of our life domains (biological, Ic, home, and social) are always in flux. One day we're healthy, the next day we're sick. Some years are professionally fruitful, and some years are not. Sometimes our social lives are busy, and other times they're not. The same goes for everyone, no matter how it might appear to you. No amount of privilege—health, wealth, good looks, education, fame, you name it—can protect a human being from struggle within life's domains.

So one of the first steps in understanding how you're being perceived is to see more clearly where you're coming from. And what is most important to remember is that no matter where you're coming from, it's 100 percent OK. Things happen in life. You're working at your I-M, the best you can in any moment given the circumstances in your domains, and so is everyone else. Let's take the story of Eric. His experience and actions illustrate what can happen when we postpone facing our challenges with honesty.

After his mother caught him using heroin, Eric was admitted to an adolescent drug treatment program I directed. He swore that he'd used heroin only four times, and he recounted each one to me in our initial meeting. In fact, he was using so much he had become addicted. He had actually gone through withdrawal the weekend before he came to my program, while he was locked up in a holding cell awaiting an appearance in court. He had had the sweats, muscle cramping, nausea, vomiting, all the incredibly uncomfortable responses of a body dramatically demanding heroin to ease the distress.

But he couldn't get any sitting in jail, and by the time he got to us, the worst of his physical symptoms had passed. He no longer needed detoxification, but the work was just beginning. My patient was not only lying about his drug use: he was lying to himself about what was happening at home, using drugs as a way to numb the pain happening in his home domain, at least temporarily if artificially.

Eric's mother was dying.

When we explored how he was working at his I-M, doing the best he could do in that moment—knowing he could change his behavior at any point—Eric was finally able to look at why he was using heroin: to escape the pain of losing his mom. His sixteen-year-old brain was anticipating times when he would be alone and roiling in fear of what life would be like without her. He identified how he sought drugs to substitute, at least for a moment, "pleasure" for pain. As he began to explore the high price he was paying for this illusory pleasure, his I-M shifted. He began to recognize that he was prematurely separating himself from his mother. And not just physically. He was painting himself as a loser, a heroin addict, a person who did not deserve her care. On another level, he was angry with her for leaving him, and attempting to punish her by his drug use: what kind of a mother has a kid that does drugs? Not a good one, he was thinking.

By understanding that his I-M could in fact change when he was ready to change it, Eric understood the lie he was telling himself. In fact, he had been lying to his mother, and then to me, because he really *did care* what people thought about him.

His ToM was very much intact. If he didn't care how his mom saw him, why would he hide using heroin at all? Why would he deny it?

He knew how his heroin use would affect his mother, and he knew how heroin users are viewed in general, as untrustworthy people. Eric did not want to be seen this way, even though he was creating that impression and was beginning to see himself that way: as a person with little value who should not be trusted. At the same time, he didn't like that he was using heroin and didn't condone it—a frequent irony in those with addiction.

A great example of this comes from the classic children's book *The Little Prince*. In one chapter, the Little Prince meets a tippler, that is, an alcoholic. The Little Prince asks the man why he drinks: to which the tippler responds that he drinks to forget. "To forget what?" asks the Little Prince. "To forget that I drink," replies the tippler. Eric was the same. He hated using, and he hated himself for using, so he began to use to forget that he saw himself as a loser, perpetuating the very image he was trying to change.

As you read this, you might be thinking, "Well, this doesn't relate to me; I'm not a drug addict." In this case, Eric's addiction shows how circumstances in one domain can cause us to make adjustments, good and bad, which can trigger a domino effect into other domains. In his life, Eric faced a struggle, the death of his mother. His choice to use heroin was an escape from the truth. The addiction then created a whole host of other problems, adversely affecting how others began to see him and, in turn, affecting how he saw himself (ToM). I've had patients struggling with obesity, divorce, job loss, mental health issues—you name it—and you can easily replace those circumstances with addiction. The lie we tell ourselves to camouflage or numb the struggles in our domains will not lead us to make the best decisions for ourselves, nor will those subsequent results improve how others see us.

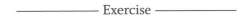 Exercise

DOMAINS, DECISIONS, AND DOMINOES

Look through the list of circumstances in the left-hand column on the next page, all of which fall within the four domains. Circle the ones you've experienced. In the second list, circle the decisions you made or actions resulting from these challenges, good and bad. If you made a poor choice at some point, did it cause you to lie to others and/or to yourself? Think about others you know whom you may have judged—or are still judging—for making similar choices.

Circumstances	Actions
Job loss	Use alcohol or drugs
Relationship breakup	Overeat
Health issue	Join a gym
Bankruptcy	See a therapist
Failed exam	Get extra help
Crashed car	Start meditation
Depression	Get on antidepressants
Rejection	Start smoking
Arrest/legal troubles	Act violently toward self or others

The I-M Approach reduces the need to lie, inasmuch as you can see yourself (and others can also see you) as doing the best you can, even if it means not living up to some preconceived standard of perfection. (Remember, it really is true that nobody's "perfect," but we are always at our I-M.) If we all want to be valued by another person, then it's possible that we'll tell "white" lies to increase that value. Sometimes these lies will serve to tell another person of your value. Sometimes these lies will be to oneself, not always with intended consequence.

Eric's story has a bittersweet conclusion. As he began to believe in the respect the treatment group had for him, his sense of value for himself was rekindled, and he began to trust again. Over a few weeks, he was able to look at himself honestly, without lying, and without fear of being rejected and kicked out of the group. In one session, he began to weep, angry with himself that he was succumbing to these emotions. He felt he needed to be strong for his mother—the mother he wanted to tend to and care for. He berated himself for being so selfish as to use heroin, and he swore he would be there for his mom.

As we explored his lying and the growing honesty that was replacing it, he was also able to recognize that *not* crying was a form of dishonesty. He took a chance later that week and cried openly with his mom at one of their family sessions, sobbing about how afraid he was to lose her. The two wept together in their pain over the truth they had to face. It was the first step in rebuilding trust, and now Eric felt he could be honest without fear of being devalued and rejected. Both of them were seeing each other at an I-M, unafraid.

The I-M Approach suggests that at a given moment, lying seems the best you can do. But with the potential to change in the very next second, one can now wonder why we feel we have to lie—at that moment or at all. Why must we feel we have to preserve an illusion?

We lie in fear of being kicked out of a powerful and protective group: either our home or a group within our social domain. And being part of a group requires one to be trusted. But nobody ever said that you can't be part of a group when you have struggles and circumstances to overcome. These are the very times to reach out to the group for help and understanding, especially when you've shown you can be trusted.

We now can see how being honest actually provides a greater chance of maintaining, if not increasing, one's value. Could you in fact be more trusted if you lied less often? Liars, once discovered, are not trusted, and lack of trust brings with it a limited access to resources and relationships and a loss of the connection we need.

Being honest actually shows courage, strength, integrity, and self-confidence in willing to be "wrong," of having had an I-M of "less-than" in others' eyes, though only temporarily. I am influencing your brain all the time, just as you are influencing mine. We can learn to make that a way to connect with each other—to belong, the subject of the next chapter.

3

Membership

THE NEED TO BELONG

Bean could see the hunger in their eyes. Not the
regular hunger, for food, but the real hunger,
the deep hunger, for family, for love, for belonging.
—**Orson Scott Card,** *Ender's Shadow*

Please accept my resignation. I don't want to belong
to any club that will accept people like me as a member.
—**Groucho Marx**

Carlos, a thirty-three-year-old patient, was so afraid of being rejected by women that for a number of years he was reluctant to even try asking anyone out. But now there was a woman in his office who had been friendly and kind to him. She had surprised him with some homemade cookies one day, and they shared a joke after a staff meeting. He thought she might be interested in him, but was unsure if her attentions were romantic or not. What she thought about him really mattered to him. He wondered what would happen if he read the signs wrong. If he asked her out on a date and she said no, he would feel humiliated and diminished. If she said yes, he would feel elated and empowered.

How he thought she saw him had enormous influence on his self-image. His ToM was turned way up, searching for any clue to how she really felt. I explored with him what harm would really be done if he asked her out and she said no. While he might feel bad about himself at first, he could also see how her possible rejection of him was not about his value, but was simply that he wasn't what she was looking for in a date.

The next time we met, Carlos was beaming. He had asked, she had said yes, and then she teased him about how long it took him to get the hint. Through each other's eyes they felt great. They had formed a new and intimate group with an exclusive membership of two.

MEMBERSHIP MATTERS

Romantic attraction illustrates in the extreme how Theory of Mind works in everyday life. Sending signals, getting signals, and inferring another person's intentions can be especially exciting when dating and building new relationships. We focus a lot of attention in this area because having others see us as valuable is so rewarding, especially when romantic feelings are in play. But even when they're not, when we feel valued by others we feel connected, and we feel we belong. Other people will look to us to gain a perception of value as well.

This dynamic has come into play even as I write this book. At times I've doubted myself, worried what other people will think of my ideas. What would a reader think if I wasn't clear? What would my editor think if I missed my deadline? I worried that I might be seen as not good enough. I feared on a deep unconscious level that I would be letting people down and would not be accepted in the protective group of people involved with this book. This kind of fear is common because, more than any kind of award or fame, we humans need acceptance and fellowship, and where we find it is for the most part in groups—our families, social circles, workplaces, cultures, tribes, religions, political parties, you name it. And in case you haven't heard, even the nerds, the prototypical outsiders, have united.

Growing up, the idea of belonging to a group is something we take for granted. We emerge from families, go to local schools, join the teams, clubs, squads, and bands. It's like breathing: without thinking, we just find ourselves there. Membership matters tremendously to kids, though they're not aware of it. Think about the devastation of not being picked for a team, or being teased for having acne. On a very deep and instinctive level, we know we want to belong. We just may not be able to put that desire into words until we're older. As we grow into adulthood, we start to move away from those built-in groups and create or join our own. It's only then that we begin to consciously notice how much membership means to us and why it's so important to our deeper sense of human belonging.

You've heard the expression *safety in numbers,* right? This is a modern colloquialism for a fundamental pillar of human survival. Being part of a group makes us feel safer. A few million years ago our ancestors were solitary mammals struggling to survive. But natural selection determined that humans who were part of a protective group fared better than solitaries trying to fend for themselves. Otherwise, we would still be solitary animals. One need only look at animals in the wild: most still survive by living in groups—herds, flocks, schools, colonies, and packs. Most people don't mind being alone for a little while, and alone time can be extremely restorative. But most of us also want (and often need) the protection of the group, not from wild predators, but to help us weather the storms of life.

Another critical reason we form groups is that group membership enhances our success. Other members can help us attain our goals, share our triumphs, and make connections, especially for social purposes. Shared values, shared goals, loyalty, obedience, and altruism are among the many assets we expect to share with our group members. We have evidence that these patterns of behavior most likely started millions of years ago when our ancestors formed social groups—families, communities, and tribes. It was, and still is, extremely beneficial to be able to predict what another group member might think and do, and those predictions were based on guesses about how that person thought or felt as the human brain's Theory of Mind capacity developed. Being part of a group made it easier to get food, access shelter, find a mate, and raise offspring. And it's no different today.

OUR HUMAN GROUPS

Social scientists classify groups in different ways, but the primary group we are born into is what's called a *dyad* (from the Greek for *two*): that of mother and child. It is from within this dyad that a child will begin to develop a sense of belonging, and eventually membership into something greater, a family.

Sometimes these dyads last a lifetime, like that between parent and child. Others may only last a few minutes or hours. Take a moment and try to think of as many dyads as you can. Here are some other examples: a romantic couple, a student and teacher, a boss and employee, a patient and physician, a taxi driver and passenger. We have one right now, author and reader. You will have others today. Each time you're in a dyad, you are making a connection in a group of two.

Groups are forming and disbanding all the time. Recognizing this is important and empowering, especially for those people who may be struggling to find a well-fitting group, be it a dyad or larger. For example, imagine you get seated in a restaurant. You and a waiter are about to form a small if temporary group: a person ready to order, and a waiter ready to take that order. Both of you, without even realizing it, are using ToM. The waiter passes by you without a glance. You wonder if he noticed you. Like our ancestors did millions of years ago, the limbic system (the seat of emotions in our brains) activates an emotion, perhaps some degree of anxiety or anger. Then the prefrontal cortex kicks in (that's the thinking and ToM part of our brains), this time wondering about our value to this new stranger, the waiter. Did his passing you by mean he didn't see you, preserving your value? Or did he purposefully ignore you, signaling your unimportance to him?

But if you're wondering about your value to him, he's also wondering about his value to you. When that waiter finally gets to your table, he may wonder whether you are annoyed or have been patient. How he treats you, the first words he says, will leave an impression: someone who apologizes and recognizes your value, or someone who is dismissive, as if your time and business don't matter. At the end of the meal, you evaluate how well the waiter served you. Did he make you feel your dining experience mattered? The best waiters do, and you send a message of that waiter's value through the tip you leave. Good waiters are empathic and want you to be a very happy member of your dyad and the restaurant, so you will return and renew your membership at another meal.

Dyads are like sparks; they can happen randomly every day. A dyad may not even entail eye contact, but even then, ToM is still activated. For example, when you're driving and another car cuts you off, that's a dyad. The other driver seems not to care at all about your point of view and can seem stupid and selfish. When you're on the phone trying to resolve an issue with your credit card company or insurance company, the agent on the phone has formed a spontaneous dyad with you. How that person treats you as a customer can have an enormous influence on how satisfied you may feel about the outcome of your discussion. Sometimes the phone rings and you hear a person asking a survey question or trying to sell you something. You may hang up, feeling intruded upon in the confines of your home, thwarting an attempted dyad. In each and all of these instances, we are still seeking to be treated with respect, even if we're going to belong to that spontaneous group for just a few minutes. When you are shown respect, you are being valued, and vice versa. Our ToM is on alert, as is the person's who forms the other half of that dyad.

▶ **BETTER LIVING THROUGH CHEMISTRY—
THE NATURAL KIND**

Membership is really built on trust. It feels great to be around someone you trust, someone you can rely on. That's because when you see that trusted person, your brain triggers a natural "feel-good" chemical neurotransmitter. Remember oxytocin, the cuddle hormone? Oxytocin makes us feel really good, binding us to one another as members of a group. Think of those times you were at a crowded event and amid hundreds of faces, you finally see one you know well. You relax. When it's a person you're very close to emotionally, the oxytocin effect is even more powerful. In fact, members of couples that communicate well have more oxytocin than couples that don't, and they actually heal quicker from things like blisters.

What do you feel when you see a picture of your loved one's face? A rush? A sense of pleasure, calm, or joy? That's the effect of oxytocin flowing through your brain and body just at the sight of that face. This is no accident.

Oxytocin contributes to romantic bonds by increasing the attractiveness and value of your partner over all others. While this might sound like oxytocin acts as some kind of love potion, studies show that oxytocin enhances the already existing attraction, but doesn't necessarily create the attraction.

Dyad of Parent and Child

Any reader who is a parent will know about that amazing feeling you get when you first meet your new child. And any reader who was a child will know the longing we have to be loved by our parents. In evolutionary terms, this critical bond was imperative for survival in a hostile world of predators. A child who feels loved is a secure child. And as they grow older, secure children do better in the relationships they form themselves.

In this dyad, the mother takes the lead. Close contact between a mother and her infant is crucial in forging this new group and especially critical for the development of parental attachment. These were the powerful findings of a team from the University of Cologne in Germany who looked at mothers of sixty-two very-low-birth-weight babies. These pre-term babies were taken right after delivery to the neonatal intensive care unit for medical stabilization. The mothers who were able to be with their infants within three hours after birth had more secure attachments with their babies than mothers who didn't see their infants until later. Scientists have known for years about the dangers to infant development when they are deprived of attachment. The adoptions by Westerners of Romanian orphans who had barely been held during the first year of life brought to light a great awareness of attachment conditions, and the critical importance of life's first dyad.

The Love Dyad

Carlos, whom we met at the top of this chapter, was on his way into a love dyad. It's one of the most powerful groupings among our species, in case you were wondering. Do you remember the intensity of your first crush or love interest? Just think of all the love songs, sonatas, poems inspired by this group of two. This dyad goes back to ancient Adam and Eve, Romeo and Juliet, Anthony and Cleopatra, Bonnie and Clyde, and, yes, Homer and Marge, for you Simpsons fans. In movies, TV shows, books, plays, and musicals, we journey with the romantic couple from their first courtship to their sometimes tragic end.

To be in this kind of dyad, however, is different from other kinds. It's much deeper and the expectations are greater. Couples in a love dyad expect more from their relationship, so ToM needs to be engaged constantly, especially in the beginning. If we are in a love dyad, how do we see ourselves through our partner's eyes? Do we feel valued by our partner? Does it feel great to be around them because they make us feel great? Are we doing the same for our partner? Do we let them know we believe in them, that we think they are amazing? Do we tell them we love them every chance we get? When we believe in each other and value each other, we solidify our membership in this dyadic group. It helps to remind ourselves how lucky we are to have a partner like that, and we do whatever it takes to keep them close.

From an evolutionary perspective, this dyad with the potential to make babies takes on a special importance. From couples like this emerge families, so the stakes are very high when it comes to an accurate assessment of your partner's intentions. The home domain you create will have an influence on the I-M of your children.

▶ **I-M IMPACT: HOW TO HANDLE REJECTION**

I've met lots of men and women like Carlos—afraid of romantic rejection. I was afraid myself before I met my wife, out in the world trying to find the right match. It's perfectly normal to feel that sting when a certain girl or guy isn't interested in you. Your Ic domain (self-image) takes a hit, and you immediately blame yourself. You might even feel annoyed because perhaps your interpretation of signals was off, and ToM was overridden by wishful thinking. When you decide to internalize and blame the rejection on yourself, it can affect your other domains as well. You might feel nausea, even physical pain or anger so it has a domino effect on your biological domain. That anger or malaise could then affect your social domain: you're suddenly rude to a co-worker, or you start to cry in a bathroom stall. These reactions are all human and normal.

But if you apply the I-M Approach to this situation, you can choose to look at rejection in so many other ways, none of which has anything to do with who you are as a total human being. At any given moment, both you and the other person are at an I-M. Issues in the other person's various domains could influence this current maximum potential, such as their own Ic domain (self-image) or social domain. The fact that they don't see you as a potential romance has to do with *their* I-M, not yours. Most of the time, a "no" is for the best: the timing isn't right, the chemistry isn't right, the Ic of one or both isn't right, or any number of reasons. Taking the blame for rejection helps nobody. Blaming the other person helps nobody. Try acknowledging you're just at an I-M, and so is the other person, one that can change at any moment. The sting doesn't need to turn into a blister.

Membership in the Home Domain

After dyads, a group can take on any size. Membership in the home domain envelops our lives as children, and the types of relationships we have there leave a legacy lasting well into adulthood, even as we make our own families. Parents have a particular relationship with each other, and a different one with each of their children. Siblings have different relationships with each other. In a family of two parents (A and B) and two children (C and D), eleven interpersonal dynamics are in progress: (1) both parents with each other, (2) parent A with child C, (3) parent A with child D, (4) parent A with both children, (5) both parents with both children, (6) both parents with child C, (7) both parents with child D, (8) parent B with both children, (9) parent B with child C, (10) parent B with child D, and (11) both siblings with each other. My wife and I have four children, so that's a lot of Theory of Mind going on!

Many people tend to take being part of a family for granted. It's only when membership in this group can't be achieved that we see the tremendous importance the home domain holds for both individual development and emotional support. Such is the case for children in the foster care system. I've worked with children who have been in so many foster homes that they wake up some mornings not knowing where they are. They have to learn the idiosyncrasies of each new home and the personalities of the foster family members, and try to integrate as best they can.

When I was medical director of the child and adolescent outpatient clinic at McLean Hospital in Belmont, near Boston, my colleagues and I formed one of the only group therapies specifically for foster children. There they began to share their stories, not just of the abuse or neglect that led them into foster care, but what the experience of being a foster child was like.

The ones who did best were the ones who felt integrated into their new families. How this happened was fairly universal: a foster parent supported them, saw them as valuable, spent time with them, and was aware and sensitive to the conflict so many of these children faced. Having a warm and loving foster parent reminded them of their disrupted biological families, so some of the children had enormous difficulty accepting love and warmth, feeling that they were betraying their biological parents.

A group of researchers and clinicians from the University of Delaware developed an approach to work with foster children, trying to correct for the early adversity these children had experienced. They called their method the Attachment and Biobehavioral Catch-up (ABC), aimed at helping parents adapt their responses to best help their preschool foster children. The approach worked. Parental sensitivity, secure attachment, and frequent, coordinated attention resulted in children with better ToM abilities compared to other foster children who hadn't received the intervention. A child who feels valued becomes more interested in knowing what other people think or feel in general.

Children who don't feel valued stop seeking value from others, which leads (subconsciously) to a self-fulfilling prophecy of their worst nightmare. Not only do they stop seeking value, but they begin to devalue the people around them, driving them further away and reinforcing their self-image of not being good enough to be valued in the first place. But using the I-M Approach, a foster parent can recognize that this is the child's current "maximum" and not take it personally. Instead, the foster parents can keep treating the child with respect and value anyway. Eventually even the most recalcitrant child gets a reactivated ToM, begins to feel valued once again, and reciprocates in kind.

Badly behaving and difficult children can also influence parents, making them feel inadequate and not particularly valuable. Many parents I work with whose children are struggling with mental health or addiction problems think they've done something wrong, and that's why their child is doing so poorly. They need encouragement from other parents, family members, and friends to not blame themselves.

Indeed, the parents who do the best in these situations turn out to be those who feel valued and supported. South Korean researchers at Kyungpook National University sustained this observation. They studied parents who had difficult children. Some parents responded with negative behaviors, acting cold or withdrawing from a difficult child. Others were warm and responsive. Reviewing the results of the 2,130 mothers of fourteen-month-old infants, the researchers saw a significant pattern emerge: the mothers who withdrew from their child were more likely to have conflict in their marriage, to have less support from their spouse in parenting, and to be depressed, and they generally viewed themselves as less capable. In contrast, mothers who had less conflict in their marriage, more co-parenting, and more family support were less depressed and viewed themselves as more capable. The scientists added that the approach toward the child was independent of family income, whether the mother was employed in addition to being a mom, or the gender of the child.

In essence, mothers who felt more valuable had an easier time managing a difficult kid. The children were too young to appreciate their impact on their moms. But the mothers who did not feel valuable to their spouse, or others in their home and social domains, had fewer internal resources to mobilize with a difficult kid. Being supported at home or in the rest of the social world implies that you are seen as valuable, being treated with respect, and leads you to feel safer in your group. With this resource at your back, it is easier to manage difficult kids, and even difficult adults.

▶ I-M IMPACT: HOME, HEARTH, AND HEART

Do you love going home for a holiday family reunion, or do you dread it? The way you see yourself in the family dynamic is influencing that feeling. Do you feel accepted as valuable, or mostly accepted? Do you think some members wish perhaps you had done a little better in your career or love life, but just aren't saying it? Even if they are saying it, remember, that's their I-M, their own current maximum. You don't have to take it personally. Because you are also at an I-M, doing the best you can. Using the I-M Approach—knowing that each of us is doing the best we can in each moment, with the potential and option to change—family reunions can be a great source of support and fun, just the way a family is meant to be, and not a competitive endeavor where people are comparing so-called successes and counting failures.

Even within the home domain there are different degrees of membership, and different group sizes. Some kids may think their sibling is the favorite. Some kids feel more "understood" by one parent or the other. Some siblings feel closer to one sibling than another. How parents get along and how their relationship is perceived influence the integrity of the home domain. Keep an eye out for these patterns of group dynamics. These relationships can last a lifetime, long after the children are grown and have families of their own. Where do you fit into this scheme? Where do you want to fit? And how can you use ToM to make it work for you?

Consider your own family. Did your parents work together as a team? If you are a parent, how much support do you get? How valuable do you feel, not just to your children but also to the rest of your "tribe"? How many times does someone let you know you are doing a great job as a parent? How many times do you let your partner know that he or she is doing a great job? So often we take our families for granted. If this is you, try something else. See what happens when you let someone know his or her effort is valued.

As I remind people all the time, "small changes have big effects" and "you control no one but influence everyone."

MEMBERSHIP IN THE SOCIAL DOMAIN

The combination of relationships and memberships outside the family can multiply in the social domain. Mostly these affiliations are based on the group we belong to, be it our school, our workplace, a team we play for or root for, or a community club. Impactful fellowship and value in the social domain often take place within smaller groups, even dyads. For instance, when a student is valued and viewed as capable by a teacher, that student excels. Speaking from personal experience, as a child psychiatrist in-training I was called in to treat a five-year-old boy who had been abused. His mode of play during our sessions included violent make-believes with animals and puppets. I was unsure what to do in response and felt stupid and overwhelmed. How was I meant to help this troubled little boy, and how was I meant to know if I even had helped him?

My supervisor said, "Joe. You are ignorant, not stupid." At first I felt worried I had let my teacher down. But then she explained that I was just learning, so how was I meant to know what to do? Ignorant, not stupid. I would be able to learn. With just a few words, my self-esteem was rescued, and I was able to work with my teacher on how to be most effective at treating my young patient. Research shows that teachers who have high expectations of their students have students who live up to those high expectations. But teachers who don't see their students as capable and have low expectations wind up with students who achieve less.

We can see this same value phenomenon in the workplace. When employees feel their needs matter, they have been shown to be both more loyal and more productive. This doesn't necessarily mean providing employees with volleyball courts and organic cafeteria meals, like at the tech start-ups. Through ToM, people know when they're included and valued. Even providing basic lifestyle accommodations to employees can reward the employer in the long run. The research strongly bears this out. West Virginia University researchers surveyed 194 employers on the benefits of implementing workplace accommodations for employees such as buying equipment and changing work schedules. Employers reported positive outcomes: better retention of qualified employees, increased worker productivity, cost savings through fewer new employee trainings, improved interactions with co-workers, higher company morale, and increased company productivity. The direct monetary benefits of having made workplace accommodations? More than $1000.

Exercise

I-M A MEMBER?

What groups do you belong to in the social domain? Your block committee? Community board or PTA? The garden club? Are you black or white, rich or poor, Democrat, Republican, Independent, Socialist, Communist, Libertarian? Are you Muslim, Jewish, Catholic, Buddhist, Wiccan, agnostic, atheist? Are you male or female or transgender? Straight, gay, or bisexual? Are you a fan of Sherlock Holmes or *Game of Thrones* or *The Walking Dead?* Your profession is also a group, along with associations, like unions, that support these professions.

Each of these groups requires one thing: that you identify with other members of that group and they with you. What values do you share with your fellow group members? How do you know you are part of that group to begin with? You may be surprised how much diversity can be found within the same group. For example, there are no religious restrictions to being a Red Sox fan.

In each of your groups, make a mental note of where you think you fit in the group's structure or hierarchy. If you're content, can you assess how you got there? If not content, how do people think and feel about you and how do those impressions contribute to your place in the hierarchy? Each of those impressions is under your influence. What action do you need to take so those impressions change and you can move toward a different status as a group member? For example, the small change of getting to work 30 minutes early can have the big effect of getting a jump on the day. Your increased productivity is sure to be noticed.

If you don't feel valued in these groups no matter what changes you make, maybe it's time to look into a few others that better align with your interests, ideas, and passions.

Groups can blend and merge, cross over, or be rigidly divided. Most of us are in more than one group at a time. For example, I am a Red Sox fan. I have friends who are Yankee fans (yes, I really do). All of us are baseball fans. My son is a soccer fan, and he and I and all those baseball fans are sports fans. Groups can be based on geography like cities and towns, countries, and continents. And within those large geographies are other groups like ethnicities or religious affiliations, political parties, genders. The Internet offers unlimited group-making opportunities. You get the idea.

Usually we want to be part of a group whose beliefs and values we share. The way we know we share these values is through ToM. To do this we blend the part of the brain that identifies us as an individual with another part of the brain that scientists call the "social brain." Brain scans actually show the close relation between the two brain areas identified with the personal and social selves.

In 2012, researchers at the University of Queensland used functional magnetic resonance imaging (fMRI) to observe the interplay between this social brain and parts of the brain traditionally thought to be involved in the "personal self" and ToM. The results of their study, published in the journal *Neuropsychologia*, suggest we derive our self-image from the groups we belong to. So it follows that how we see ourselves depends significantly on what we think *other people* think we are. For instance, if someone says we're conservative because we're registered a Republican, or a nature lover because we live in the country, it actually encourages us to believe those things about ourselves. You probably make the same assumptions about others. Take a moment and consider what others might think about you based on a group you're in that simply isn't true.

▶ MEMBERS ONLY

Have you ever been to a social gathering where you find some people you just love talking with, much more than the others who are there? Notice why? It's not just because they may be attractive. It's usually because they seem to really "get" you, and you "get" them. They make eye contact, listen to your stories attentively, laugh or nod at the right time, or reach out and pat your arm as a gesture of understanding. These kinds of people help you feel like a welcome, important part of the group. Their empathetic response makes you feel great, and you want to be around them even more. What they have done is tap into your own ToM, probably without even knowing that's what they're doing.

People with highly active ToM are more likely to have a high "EQ," or *emotional quotient,* a measurement of emotional intelligence. The EQ concept was brought into public awareness in 1995 with the publication of psychologist Daniel Goleman's book *Emotional Intelligence.* It refers to the ability to monitor one's own and other people's emotions, to carefully discern different emotions and label them appropriately, and to use emotional information to guide thinking and behavior. Studies have shown that a higher EQ predicts career satisfaction and success, and even higher incomes compared to lower-EQ counterparts. What's at the root of EQ? Theory of Mind.

So now you know the basic mechanism of how the human mind operates, and you can use it any time you want. In a social gathering where many people might not know anyone, you can already imagine how most people are feeling. Think about it. They feel just like you do—in need of making a connection so they feel part of the group.

Try this exercise: Turn on the TV or pull up YouTube, and watch a clip of a TV show or movie with the sound off. See if you can figure out, just by looking at the faces and body

posture of the actors, what they are feeling, which character feels part of the group, and which one may feel left out of
the group. Watch it again with the sound on to see how accurately you guessed. The better you are at understanding what
someone else is thinking or feeling, the better you'll be at making someone feel a member of the group you may just start
yourself.

Religious Membership

These are not boom days for membership in the various religions
in the United States. According to a 2012 Pew Research Center
poll, the number of Americans who don't identify with any religion continues to rise. As of 2012, a fifth of the U.S. public, and a
third of adults under thirty, categorize themselves as religiously
unaffiliated. This group has actually been called "nones." Thus, a
new group, ironically, is created.

Karl Marx was disdainful of religion, calling it the "opium of
the people." But from a brain point of view, this remarkable bond
between people has served a critical purpose in our development:
it has eased our fear of death and encouraged us to strive for higher
ideals. Many religions teach that our actions in this life will be the
basis of our value in the next. It feels very, very comforting to be
part of a group with such a powerful protective force. So while
membership in traditional religions may be on the decline, the
sense of community and spirituality that the church, temple, and
mosque used to have a monopoly over remains influential.

Membership in a spiritual group can provide a powerful sense
of belonging, of value, and of faith, which is the enactment of
trust. There is compelling evidence that people who believe in
something greater than themselves actually heal faster and have
fewer medical problems to begin with. With modern brain map-

ping technology like MRI, scientists now can get a picture of what is actually happening in our individual brains when we function as members of a spiritual group.

For example, researchers from the National Institute on Aging, a division of the National Institutes of Health, used sophisticated brain imaging techniques to map regions of the brain involved in religious thought. In a provocative 2014 paper titled "Brain Networks Shaping Religious Belief," investigators showed how the prefrontal cortex and Theory of Mind were intimately involved in processing religious thought which they referred to broadly as "supernatural agents," meaning God, knowledge of doctrine, how beliefs related to everyday life, and fear and emotion regulation. The perception of these agents they wrote, "engaged pathways involved in fear regulation and affective ToM." In fact, perceiving oneself allied with any group activates the prefrontal cortex. Affiliation with a spiritual group and empathy go hand in hand, brought together through ToM.

When it comes to human mortality and life's existential questions, membership in a religion has long been a comforting place, as both answers and emotional support are made available. But those brain pathways engaged by religious and spiritual ideas don't require religious membership. A faith in a higher being can be enough "membership" for some people. I recently met with a young man who was dealing with a traumatic event that had occurred when he was seven years old. He had been in a serious car accident while driving with his family. The car was hit with such force it flipped onto its roof. He could still remember the terrifying feeling of spinning around wildly, strapped into his seat but seeing everything upside down. He crawled out of the vehicle and saw his mother bleeding and broken in the distance, as she had been thrown out of the car. His baby sister was still strapped into her car seat inside, screaming. As the police and ambulances arrived, he told them, sobbing, that his sister was trapped, and he watched as they used a jaws-of-life tool to extract her. But there were no jaws of life to save his mother.

He began a journey, moving from relative to relative, feeling increasingly isolated and unloved. Now he was living with his girlfriend, their three-year-old child, and her grandmother. He described to me an inability to trust anyone, at least "anyone human." Yet he had a strong faith in God. This was his deepest relationship, the only one he believed in. It was the only relationship in which he felt there must be some value to his life or he would not have survived the crash, which had become a metaphor for his life. He was upside down, spinning, but what kept him going was that he had forged a dyadic relationship with God.

I hear about such relationships over and over in my practice. Some people have a deep and profound relationship with their own God, finding succor and comfort being part of such a powerful and protective group. A person does not need to be part of a formal religious group to have this spiritual connection. Indeed, many people forgo the formality, and sometimes the rigid strictures of a religion, but remain highly spiritual. This young man was one of them, desperate to regain some sense of equilibrium out of the emotional chaos he had experienced since seeing his mother die in that car crash.

Gangs and Cults

The need for belonging is so powerful it can lead us into groups that, while protective to some degree, do not have the best interests of their members truly at heart. Some of the people I work with are so desperate to be accepted, or live in such dangerous environments, that they join almost any group that will take them. I'm talking now about street gangs.

According to 2012 statistics from the National Gang Center, U.S. gang members numbered about 850,000, up 8.6 percent over the previous year. The gang member represents our desperation to be included in something, with someone, no matter how nefarious.

Danny, one of my teen patients, was a gang member (and may still be). I met him when he was seventeen, one small teardrop tattooed at the corner of his right eye, more tattoos on his knuckles. He had been brutally initiated at the age of twelve. The neighborhood he lived in was a scary place, but also one where you could be protected if you knew the right people and belonged to the right group. But the price for this type of protection was high and confined to Danny's immediate "hood." Step outside the boundaries and you're in someone else's territory, an adversary of a different gang. The danger didn't bother Danny. In the gang's ranks, he had risen from soldier to lieutenant and felt powerful and safe. His gang was his main group, more important to him even than family.

A great deal is known about why teens and young adults join gangs. As with any group, gang membership can provide a sense of identity, fellowship, and brotherhood. In Danny's case, the first draw was the literal physical protection the group offered. In some cases, though, youth are forced to join after being threatened, intimidated, or beaten. Researchers cite that the main predictor for male youth joining a gang is growing up in a neighborhood with a low level of social integration. Not surprisingly, other variables include poverty, absence of biological parents, and low parental attachment and supervision. Poor academic performance and low attachment to teachers were also cited as strong risk factors.

Some of these risk factors also apply to joining cults. In a cult, obedience trumps independence. Your membership depends on how well you please the leaders of the cult, even if it means dishonoring your own family. And if you do not show obedience, you are not allowed to leave the group but are punished and shunned. Research shows that poor family structure, neglect, and poverty are key variables, along with emotional vulnerability, debilitating crises, and stress. All of these can increase a person's likelihood to turn to outside groups. It's not just the home domain: all four domains are at play. The statistics vary on the numbers of young adults joining cults, but they're considerably higher than those joining gangs. Research by behavioral scientists at Lubbock Christian University in 2005 has indicated that between two million and five million young adults were involved in cult groups in the United States, a fairly alarming number that indicates the compelling nature of groups that promise to hold all the answers.

Shane, another of my patients, was seventeen when he joined a cult. Shane told me he'd never felt like he fit in anywhere, until one day he met a girl. She told him she had felt the same way in her life, but was now part of a big and welcoming family. After a few weeks, she took him to her house and introduced him to some of her friends, who also welcomed him warmly. For the first time, Shane felt he belonged. He felt special, part of a larger, more spiritual community. But the cost of membership of this new group had repercussions: he had left home, dropped out of school, and was now handing out pamphlets on the streets. "That's my job," he reported proudly. His parents sat flanking him in my office. They were not hiding their distress, which had been conveyed during the session in wrenching sobs from Shane's mother. Shane had switched membership from his family to one in which he felt valuable, doing, he thought, spiritual work for the good of many.

▶ **I-M IMPACT: BLENDER OR AMENDER?**

In any group, you're bound to see a hierarchy in place, albeit a fluid one. Any group usually includes what I call *blenders* and *amenders*. Blenders follow the rules and agenda set by amenders. Some people might refer to this structure as leaders and followers, but only truly type A people are compelled into the leader category all the time. Each of us takes on both of these roles every day, depending on the group one is in. For instance, at home my wife is the amender and I'm a blender. But at work it's different. It's my job to set the agenda. These roles are dynamic and changing all the time, just as your I-M changes in response to changing stimuli in the four domains.

Perhaps you'd like to change your status in certain groups. You now know enough about Theory of Mind to shift group members' perception of you. Try keeping track of how you think you're perceived within your groups. For example, if you're going out for dinner with your family or friends, how is the restaurant chosen? At work, if you're collaborating on a team project, how does that project get done? How does your view of another team member influence the role you take as an amender or blender? How does team members' view of you influence the role you are given? Both amenders and blenders have value to the group: which role do you generally prefer and why? Whether you're in the role of a blender or an amender, you're at your I-M—doing the best you can in each moment—but you have the opportunity to change circumstances in your domains by using ToM.

LOYALTY AND MEMBERSHIP

If you've ever been around young children playing with each other, you'll soon notice that they don't actually play together at all. Young children play side by side in what is called *parallel play*. As children get older they begin to interact, and play becomes more of a communal activity. Go to a playground and you'll see some kids playing with each other, creating all sorts of games and taking on all sorts of roles. Some are the heroes, some the villains. Sometimes teams are formed, and a child spontaneously becomes a member of that playgroup. Immediately, certain expectations of membership come about, and one of them is loyalty. Have you ever seen a play session where one kid is perceived as disloyal because he broke an unspoken rule? Chaos can erupt.

A research group from the Max Planck Institute for Evolutionary Anthropology in Leipzig, Germany, wanted to know at what age this expectation of loyalty starts. The researchers recruited twenty-four girls and twenty-five boys with an average age of five years from local day-care centers. The children were shown videos of two groups of female actors competing against each other to build towers out of plastic cups. After the contest, two of the girls from the losing team were interviewed. One of the girls was loyal to her group and said she would stick with them. The other girl basically said she was in a group of losers and couldn't wait to dump them and go into the other group. The observing children were then asked a series of questions: which of the girls was nicer, doing the right thing, more trustworthy, deserved a reward, and which girl their teammates didn't like anymore. The five-year-olds preferred loyal to disloyal teammates.

Surprisingly, the observing children responded this way even though they were not part of the groups themselves. When someone is loyal to you, you trust them more, like them more, admire them more, and want to reward them more so they remain part of your group.

The researchers repeated the same study with four-year-olds. This time the findings were not as consistent, suggesting that a four-year-old is beginning to understand loyalty but its importance has not fully jelled. Loyalty is the expected norm among children, as it is among adults, but like ToM, it's on a spectrum of development.

Think about your own life. Have you had friends who are no longer friends? What did they do—or what did you do—to lose that trust? What types of disloyalty were displayed? In all relationships, loyalty is required. Without loyalty there is no trust. In marriage, disloyalty can lead to divorce if trust isn't rebuilt. Trusting someone makes you feel less anxious, and anxiety is a very uncomfortable feeling that makes you want to hide or run away. When you trust someone, your brain releases oxytocin, a very different chemical and a much nicer feeling.

How do you measure someone's loyalty? Your answer to that question will help you choose the people you want around you, because you want to be in a group with shared values. Team loyalty, school loyalty, family loyalty: these loyalties bind us together. And when someone is bound to you in this way, everyone feels safer. From a ToM point of view, you have again reassured someone of your value, and that feels great.

Group Strength

Back in 1935, two men began a friendship that has grown into one of the world's greatest examples of the power of membership. When Bill W. and Dr. Bob began to talk with each other about their alcoholism, they were just two men who had formed a small group, a fellowship built around their mutual struggle with alcohol addiction. Now that founding dyad has grown into thousands of groups of millions of members all over the world: Alcoholics Anonymous. To become a member, all you need is a desire to be sober. That's it: you're in, and you're accepted.

If you've ever been to an AA meeting, the warmth and acceptance of new members can be extremely powerful to witness. In my adolescent addiction program, we meet in this kind of setting almost every night. Members of AA and NA (Narcotics Anonymous) join the current patients to talk about their journey through the seduction, addiction, and recovery from drugs and alcohol. These volunteers give their time to come and share their stories, a healing process for them and for my patients. Some of the most powerful stories come from teens who went through my program, and then come back as a group to tell about their journeys. They are truly inspiring.

The cohesion and sense of belonging provided through the AA and NA experience have spread worldwide in the last half-century, giving members strength to overcome their addiction. In the United States, and in some other countries such as Sweden, for instance, AA and similar support groups are the most frequently endorsed treatment for alcoholism.

Being a member of a group can help with many other addictions and health matters, even quitting smoking. Even one key supporter can make a big difference. A study from South Carolina recruited smokers who chose one of two groups—one that intended to "quit now" or another to "quit later." Of the 1,132 participants, those who were ready to quit now had more support from their significant others than those who placed themselves in the "quit later" group.

Having someone else help you in any way increases your sense of value through the eyes of significant others: perhaps the reason the folks in the "quit now" group were ready to do so. The health risks of cigarettes are well-known. But recognizing one's value to someone else appears to be a very strong incentive to quit. We take a similar focus at my adolescent substance abuse program. We help our kids regain their sense of value by treating them with respect, activating their Theory of Mind capabilities, which leads them to trust, to begin to explore their addiction without judgment, and to move away from drugs and alcohol. They have become a member of a group, in this case a group of sober kids and adults who care about them—a pathway to rekindling their sense of value.

Group Identity

We enjoy being with other people who are like us in some way. Sharing a particular skill or interest forms the foundation of many groups, and this ability to form a group can happen quickly and spontaneously. When it does, members of the new group develop a loyalty to each other that can rapidly create emotional walls around the group, a side effect of membership called *bias*. You've seen this no doubt among fans of sports teams. The sports analogy is black and white—you're either with us or you're not. But the phenomenon is built into the whole concept of membership.

Most academic experiments studying group behavior involve strangers who are placed by scientists in different experimental conditions. The study conditions are designed to mimic real everyday life as closely as possible. That was the goal of an Australian research team from the Queensland Brain Institute who wanted to explore this idea of "in-group" bias. They took forty-eight strangers and gave them a test in which they had to estimate the number of dots randomly dispersed on a page. The participants were told they'd be assigned to a red or blue team based on their guess: overestimators and underestimators. In reality, the team assignments were completely random, but these strangers felt they had something in common with their other team members. For the rest of the day-long study, red team members wore red jackets, and blue team members wore blue jackets.

The red and blue teams were then pitted against each other in a contest. Participants sat at a computer screen and were told to reach out and press a button with their right hand as quickly as possible after hearing the word "go." Their time would be compared to the other team's time. After the button was hit, the screen would display the word "Checking…" then either "Red Wins" or "Blue Wins." In reality, the results had been randomized so that each player would "win" half the time. The scientists had easily created a sense of group membership: first by similar dot-counting ability, then by wearing the same color, and then by working as a team against another by pushing a button as fast as possible. The color represents the team, and the dot-counting their shared goal and value.

The next part of the test looked at team bias: would people see their teammates as doing better than their opponents, even if the actual results were exactly the same? To test this idea, the scientists had half the team members watch a video, each independently of the others. Each observer compared the hand-actions of two people—one wearing a blue jacket and one wearing red—reaching out as fast as possible to touch a button, then returning their hands to a resting position. (The video had been edited so that the scientists controlled the actual timing of the hand movements, always making them exactly equal.) The observer was then asked which hand was faster in completing the task.

The scientists then took the other half of the team and had them respond to the same videos, but this time while undergoing an fMRI that tracked the activity of the various areas of the brain. The result: each team member perceived his or her own teammates as being faster than their opponents.

All the subjects were then given a standard test to find out if they identified more with their group than the other. Participants were shown a photograph of a team member or opponent while also viewing a pleasant word (such as *honest, loyal, friend, happy*) or an unpleasant one (*enemy, evil, rotten, hatred*). Team members responded more quickly to pleasant words when paired with teammates' pictures, and unpleasant words when paired with opponents' pictures. Seeing a pleasant word with an opponent's picture, or an unpleasant word with a teammate's picture created an incongruity and a delayed response.

With the corroborating fMRI images, this fascinating study showed how our brains have actually developed to believe that members of "our" group perform better than people who are not in our group.

Groups are biased. They have to be. To me what is amazing and unspoken about this and other group-behavior experiments is how quickly a bunch of strangers can identify themselves as a group at all. Our deeply rooted competitive brains want our team to be better than our rival team. This bias can form very quickly, as it did with the people on the red and blue teams who attributed superiority to their team members over their opponents. Because it feels so good to be valued like this, people in that group keep coming back for more mutual support, and the group stays together.

—————— Exercise ——————

BIAS BY US

No one really wants to be seen as biased because it implies something negative about us. Since negativity could decrease our value in the eyes of others, we try to avoid bias. But it happens all the time, most often unconsciously. As you saw with the Australian red-blue team study, our brains are designed to favor our team members' skills and appearance. It feels good to be a member of a powerful and capable group of people. From a Theory of Mind perspective, this is exactly why I'd want to stay in that group: because I too could be perceived as superior.

When you can honestly look at your own bias, it gives you an insight into how this happens—not just in your brain but in everyone's brain. Let's face it: someone, somewhere, sees you as part of the inferior group (team, gender, company, culture, race, profession, nationality, and so on). Admittedly or not, that person imposes a bias onto you, and you do the same thing too.

This insight can help you access empathy, a major component of Theory of Mind. It's more than just putting yourself in someone else's shoes. It's recognizing that we're all in the *same* shoes: we all have basically the same brain capable of bias.

What biases have you had, even today? Some may be benign, such as recommending a particular favorite food or drink. But some may be more malignant, such as placing judgment or saying something negative without reflection. Do these biases really help you feel more valuable? Or do they actually diminish your value because you see other people as inferior, leaving them more likely to mistrust you?

Group Loyalty—Thicker Than Water?

Empathy is a natural extension of Theory of Mind, our ability to take someone else's perspective. If we infer that someone is struggling, we can then choose to help because we relate to that experience. We do this especially well with people to whom we feel a kinship or shared identity. In a movie, we can empathize with the jilted lover, feeling that person's pain and anguish. We can feel the excitement of discovering a treasure, the sadness of losing a loved one, the elation of winning, and the joy and passion of falling in love and having that love reciprocated.

But what happens to empathy if we *don't* identify with the other person? That was the question that scientists from the University of Rome wanted to answer. The researchers placed thirteen black African subjects from Burundi, Cameroon, Congo, Nigeria, and Tunisia and fourteen Italian white subjects in an fMRI scanner where they watched videos of right male hands being stroked gently with a cotton swab or being stabbed deeply with a hypodermic needle. The holder of the swab or needle was never revealed. Some of the hands were white, others were black, and a third set were shaded violet. Previous to the fMRI, all the subjects had taken tests to measure racial bias and how empathic they were.

After each video, the subjects were asked to rate the intensity and unpleasantness of being stroked with a cotton swab or being stabbed with a syringe. Additionally, the subjects' pupil size—an indication of an involuntary and automatic biological response to the videos—was also being monitored. What the scientists discovered was perhaps what they expected. Specific parts of the brain lit up in subjects who were more racially biased when they saw their own race being stuck with the needle. It was as if they were experiencing the pain themselves, or at least were empathizing with the person being jabbed. It was clear that all the subjects had their own racial bias, empathizing more with "in-group" members, and that specific parts of our brains are responsible for how we emotionally respond to our own pain.

The "social brain" and "individual brain" can get quite jumbled up when group identity and bias are activated. Group bias can even interfere with one's memory of performing an action. A research group from the University of Kassel in Germany randomly picked action statements—such as "open the door"—and asked fifty-eight fair-skinned German participants to perform half of the tasks and only read the other half. Next the participants watched either a video of the torso, arms, and hands of a fair-skinned German actress performing all the tasks or a video of the torso, arms, and hands of a Sri Lankan dark-skinned actress doing the same. Two weeks later the participants were asked which of the tasks they themselves had actually performed. False memories were much more pronounced for participants who had watched the fair-skinned actress performing an action, and much less for participants who had watched the dark-skinned person performing an action. The participants demonstrated no difference in false memories when they watched actions performed by a hand wearing a black glove to disguise skin color. Although they probably didn't mean to, the fair-skinned participants identified more with the fair-skinned actress. Group bias can make you believe you did something, even when you really didn't. The "social brain" can get so intertwined with the "individual brain" that people can lose perspective on the actions they take. When this happens, one group can begin to turn upon another.

No matter the religion or race, the poverty or power, we are each a member of some group, along with this vast group we call humanity. Using our Theory of Mind, we discern where we stand in these groups. And that can be very comforting. Theory of Mind may be very good at making someone feel great. Others use ToM to help you feel valued too.

But as we are really interested in what other people think or feel about *us* now it's time to explore the consequences of our interest in that subject. And this may take some courage.

4

Alienation

THE PRICE OF NOT BELONGING

"You want to know what's wrong with the world?"
Dad paused. "It's this alienation that permeates
every aspect of humanity."
—**Mark David Henderson,** *The Soul of Atlas*

All the children stood in a circle behind their little multi-colored chairs. "You guys ready?" asked the teacher. Then she turned on a catchy tune, and the kids skipped nervously around the circle. Fifteen seconds later, the teacher turned the music off, and each of the children scrambled for a chair. But there were only fourteen chairs for the fifteen children. So two kids scrambled for one last chair, with one little girl getting bumped onto the floor. Disappointed, out she went, along with one of the chairs, relegated to watching the next round. There she sat with an acute feeling of not belonging to the group as the music started up again.

There's perhaps no greater metaphor for a competitive approach to life than the game of musical chairs. Isn't it ironic that this is a game for small children? It has to be one of the most nerve-wracking games I can think of, even still to just watch. Just as easily as we can make someone feel included in a fun game, in an instant we can eliminate, exclude, and alienate. And with musical chairs, how early we prepare our young for this experience of being the outsider, if only for a few moments.

In the previous chapter, we explored membership: being chosen for inclusion either by a special person or a group of people, and how critical this is to our well-being as humans. But what happens when we're *not* welcomed into the membership, when we're left out? The kid waiting to be picked for a game of capture the flag gets a sinking feeling in the pit of his stomach when passed over; the actress doubts herself if she doesn't see her name on the cast list; the high school senior worries he'll never get into college after being rejected by several; the woman who didn't get the job she really wanted feels incompetent; a jilted lover despairs that no one will ever want to have him as a lifelong partner.

In each of these examples, recognizable to us all, the underbelly of Theory of Mind is exposed. We unconsciously care so much about what other people think of us, and of being connected to them, that we can feel blindsided when we find ourselves on the outs. We can imagine all kinds of reasons for our rejection, and we turn the experience into a commentary on our character and worth. And when this happens to us we feel the hollow ache of alienation. Yet we perpetrate alienation on each other all the time. I'm not talking here about blatant bigotry, but about our small, insidious biases, often combined with our own insecurities, that allow us to put someone else down. In the process, we're devaluing and alienating them from our group, which can be the pathway to bigotry.

Why do we do this to each other? The reasons are complex, but the results of this side of human nature, especially in the modern world, can lead to impasses and perpetuation of violence toward one another. But by using our ToM abilities consciously, we can take a first step toward ending our own feelings of alienation. As we learn more about how this works, we can help teach others to do this as well.

If you closely observe the game of musical chairs, you'll often see children shouting to support each other—a collective "Awww" is heard when someone goes out. "Hey Katie, there's a chair here!" and "Come over here, Hector," they shout, trying to help each other locate a place. The kids know there's going to be an odd person out, and they hope it's not themselves or their friends. The difference we adults need to understand better, and implement in society, is that in grown-up life we can—and I argue should—make sure there are enough chairs. When we include rather than exclude, our communities and societies are happier, more peaceful, and safer for all.

ALIENATION AND THE SEE-SAW OF VALUE

Stated simply, alienation begins when one person devalues another person. When we ignore, we devalue. When we exclude, we devalue. When we say impulsive, mean, and thoughtless words, we devalue another person. Those words and actions can deeply hurt others through the lens of ToM by signaling that they're not valued in the eyes of the person speaking those words. We alienate others on many levels—religious, societal, racial, economic, educational, and more. When we feel alienated we feel alone, scared, angry, desperate, and hopeless.

▶ **I-M IMPACT: ARE YOU AND HAVE YOU EVER BEEN AN ALIENATOR?**

Now I'm going to ask you to use the I-M Approach to do something really hard: look at yourself to see how you have alienated others. Notice I said "how," not "if." This is because we all do it. But allow yourself to acknowledge that at the time you alienated others your "I-M" (I-Maximum) may have been at an I-M you may not like or condone—perhaps you were in a hurry or in a bad mood. By using the I-M Approach, you can take responsibility and look at yourself with respect and not judgment. This acceptance and accompanying safety lets you be more honest with yourself, and you can then change to a different I-M if you don't like the current one.

How many of these things have you done yourself?

- gossiped about someone else
- teased someone to make others laugh
- criticized someone
- ignored someone's greeting or request
- failed to invite someone you should have to an event
- belittled people behind their back
- insulted someone
- lied to someone
- lied about someone to someone else

If any of these behaviors seem familiar and you can admit to them, then you have just been courageous. You might remember some of these times very distinctly because you regretted them, knowing through your ToM how you made someone feel. Maybe you apologized and maybe you didn't.

And you might remember some of these times because, in truth, they gave you satisfaction: it felt good to put someone else down. Be honest.

You can also see, again using ToM, how and why these types of alienating behaviors may have been perpetrated on you by someone else. Alienating behaviors can be subtle but very powerful because of their influence on another's sense of value. You really do control no one and influence everyone. Those small changes you make can have a big effect, and the first change may simply be seeing yourself at an I-M and others as well. Remember, everybody is at an I-M, including you, and along with it we have the opportunity to change circumstances, behaviors, and relationships at any point.

But even as we explore the outer edges of alienation, we also celebrate when the outsider becomes an insider. Over the last Christmas holidays, I was bombarded with one familiar holiday melody after another. The messages of peace and love and good will to all flooded our kitchen, the shopping mall, and the car radio. One of the songs was "Rudolph the Red-Nosed Reindeer." I apologize in advance for planting this tune in your head, but remember the tale of Rudolph? If ever there were a perfect metaphor for our back-and-forth relationship with alienating behaviors, this would be it. Read, or sing, on:

> Rudolph the red-nosed reindeer
> Had a very shiny nose
> And if you ever saw it
> You would even say it glows.

In the first verse, Rudolph is distinguished and set apart from all the other reindeer. He looks different. He has a glowing red nose. That doesn't sound too bad. But in the next verse, we learn that the other reindeer laughed at Rudolph, called him names, and wouldn't let him in on their games, essentially shunning him because he was so noticeably different. Because he didn't conform to the traditional, acceptable appearance of reindeer, he was teased and bullied. Rudolph felt different, alone, unloved, and alienated, of little or no value to his peers. When you use ToM to relate to a fictional reindeer's feelings, a startling example of alienation and bullying emerge. The good news though, as you're undoubtedly aware, is that Rudolph saved the day with his shiny nose, and then suddenly he was valued.

Why does the story of Rudolph—and many other stories like it—resonate so deeply with each of us? Because we can all relate to the feeling of being devalued by others, of being the odd one out. We also feel empathy for the lone deer, the underdog, and we cheer for him to get back "in." We also all know that we want the story to have a happy ending, and that alienation just isn't intrinsically good for anyone.

Feelings of loneliness and alienation have forever been a part of the human condition. We're born alone. We die alone. As far back as we can read, philosophers, historians, and other writers have explored this existential mystery of aloneness. Throughout human life there has always been the painful awareness of alienation from others. In a collection of essays on the subject, *Man Alone: Alienation in Modern Society*, editors Eric and Mary Josephson wrote:

> In its panorama of disorder and change, history offers plentiful evidence that men in times past also felt no small uncertainty about themselves and their identities, suffered no little anguish, gloom, despair and feeling of detachment from each other.

But in our modern world, one where science and technology are so fully integrated into daily life and where close-knit extended family has been replaced by a mobile society, we face what some would argue is a colder or less compassionate existence than we have had at any time in history. Cambridge historian Peter Laslett wrote in his frequently referenced work, *The World We Have Lost:*

> Time was, and it was all time up to 200 years ago, when the whole of life went forward in the family, in a circle of loved, familiar faces, known and fondled objects, all to human size. That time has gone forever. It makes us very different from our ancestors.

Today the experience of social alienation is all around us, embedded in everyday life: how we eat (single serving); how we live (alone or in temporary nuclear families); how we commute (single-passenger cars), and how we communicate (less and less in person, especially in these digital times). As physicians and concerned members of society, we see the results of this modern-day alienation and are committed to helping people understand what's going on, especially our youth.

For those starting families and with small children, I would argue there is a critical need to help instill in children a strong sense of connection and belonging in their developing years. Too often at our treatment center, I see the results of alienation within the family. Lack of connectedness in the family setting—the very roots of belonging for most human beings—can have disastrous effects in the young adult mind.

▶ **CULTURAL ALIENATION—THE IMMIGRANT STORY**

Aliens are by definition unfamiliar, unknown, strange, and foreign. They're big black-eyed space creatures who pose an uncertain danger to humankind. But the same word is used every day at our nation's borders, by politicians and law enforcers to describe human beings who just happen to be non-American. In the United States, we confer the status of "resident alien" on people from other countries who live here legally. On other immigrants without papers, we confer the term "illegal alien." The very nature of the word says clearly that an alien is someone who does not belong here. So by using this language, we continue to alienate.

As of this writing, the nation is galvanized into conflicting groups around what to do with illegal aliens. Do we confer citizenship on them, cut them some legal slack, or kick them out and deport them back to their country of origin? Do we expand our group by increasing our membership, or do we maintain or decrease the size of our group by excluding those we deem inadequate because they look different, speak another language, and are "alien"?

The story of immigrants to the United States has been, and still seems to be, one of alienation and hardship as they struggle for a foothold in a new land. Yet most families I know have an immigrant connection within a generation or two back. Speaking to a mainstream audience, Franklin D. Roosevelt, perhaps unwittingly using ToM, famously stated, "Remember, remember always, that all of us, and you and I especially, are descended from immigrants and revolutionists." Yet here we are today and little has changed of society's perception of "aliens."

ALIENATION AT HOME

I work every day with young patients from ages ten to eighteen. The kids who spend time with us at the treatment center come because they're struggling with the result of choices that have led them into substance abuse. Taking that first hit of weed or that first drink was a small change with a big effect. As a result of their behaviors, many of my patients feel alienated, depressed, and worthless, burdened by a sense that they have no value. Some come from stable, intact families struggling with challenges. Others come from chaotic and sometimes abusive backgrounds.

Some of the kids feel so worthless they become suicidal, convinced that the world would be a better place without them. Others fear being devalued so much that their anxiety paralyzes them from making any attempt at change. Afraid of failing, they sometimes shut down completely. Tragically, this self-isolation can spiral out of control.

One fifteen-year-old girl, whom I'll call Zoe, never felt connected to a family unit. Her father left when she was a toddler. Her mother moved around a lot, worked various jobs at all hours, and had a series of boyfriends. There were no other family members to help, and Zoe bounced from one school to another. As a result of this chaotic upbringing, Zoe never felt she belonged anywhere, even at her home, where she was usually alone. She had a hard time making friends and dwelled in negativity. When Zoe came into my office, I discovered she had scratched the word "unlovable" into her skin. At some point, Zoe's Theory of Mind abilities became hypersensitive to criticism, as she interpreted others' behavior toward her as non-accepting. The slightest hint of rejection drove her to a very dark and self-destructive I-M—her current state of doing the best she could with what she knew.

When children grow up in homes where they don't feel a sense of belonging, the psychological damage is incalculable, as is the case with many foster children. And the lasting effects on the physical health of these kids, as they grow into adulthood, are showing to be measurable in devastating ways. In one very compelling study, UCLA researchers examined if and how family background influenced people's health later in life. The study, called Coronary Artery Risk Development in Young Adults, involved 756 adults who represented a subset of more than 5,000 participants from various ethnicities, ages, and economic, educational, and geographic backgrounds.

The research showed definitively that the adults who grew up in homes where there were higher levels of verbal abuse reported more health problems like high blood pressure, increased cholesterol, diabetes, and coronary artery disease. Contrast this to adults who reported supportive and loving families, homes with warm and affectionate parents: these adults reported fewer health problems in general. This outcome adds to a wide and growing body of evidence showing how childhood maltreatment leads to dysregulation in psychobiological stress and immune system responses, which is believed to be a cause of long-term mental and physical health problems.

The mechanism cited by the researchers for this health deterioration across the less nurtured group had to do with what's called *allostatic load:* a fancy term for the wear and tear of stress on the body. Our stress response is ancient, tens if not hundreds of millions of years old, and it served us well early in our species survival, when daily life posed many threats. Today, even though we don't need to contend with saber-tooth tigers, our brains are still fine-tuned to react to potential danger, and our stress response activates in the very same powerful way. Here's how it works.

In the environment of a toxic, unpredictable, and chaotic home domain, the stress response kicks into gear and with it the brain sends a message to release cortisol, the stress hormone. Cortisol courses through the blood stream to the heart, which begins to beat faster, to the lungs, which begin to breathe more rapidly; and to the blood vessels, which constrict so the blood can travel faster under higher pressure. The body automatically pumps up its immune system, preparing to defend against any invading germs: perhaps from the saliva of a gnashing saber-tooth, or the bacteria that could infect an open wound. In the same way, the body releases proteins for more effective blood clotting so you won't bleed to death if you're bitten or injured.

All of the body's activities during the stress response take considerable energy. Faced with a shortage of energy, the body begins to hoard fat, a long-term energy source. For our ancestors, not only was physical attack a threat, so was a shortage of calories. We developed a way to store the energy from that food for later: as fat on the body.

Sugar, or glucose, is the immediate and major source of the energy needed to run our bodies. That energy has to get everywhere in the body, so glucose is carried along in the bloodstream. But to get into the cell itself, to give that cell the energy it needs to get things done, the glucose has to be moved by a special transport molecule called insulin. Under stress, the brain demands more energy than usual, so it grabs more glucose from the rest of the body. In this *brain pull* mode, the brain limits insulin in the rest of the body and instead increases sugar in the blood so it can get into the brain.

What the UCLA researchers confirmed was that the children in homes with high stress and low levels of human connection had an amped-up cortisol response, and the brain began to adapt. From the brain's point of view, the world was a dangerous place. In a dangerous place, you have to be on guard. And to be on guard you had to keep your cortisol levels higher than if you were living in a calm and nurturing home. As those children got older, the stress response stayed on in the form of a higher allostatic load, instead of being activated only in cases of emergency. Blood pressure stayed high, clotting stayed high, and the immune response became hypersensitive. The body developed obesity due to storing fat for later, heightening the risk of type two diabetes due to insulin suppression. The clotting and high blood pressure also put those adults at greater risk for heart attacks and strokes.

Beyond the biological mechanisms at work with children, the complex psychological impact can lead to low self-esteem and little sense of self-worth. Many of my patients feel insecure, worrying that they're not good enough to be loved. Similar to Zoe, they have hypersensitive ToM, as if they're on high alert, looking for criticism.

Yoshiko was one of those people. She had a great job, had bought herself a fancy car, and always wore the most fashionable clothes. But she couldn't stay in a relationship for more than a few months. Or more precisely, she couldn't keep anyone else in a relationship for more than a few months—until that day she told me she'd met someone she could stay with. He wasn't the greatest, but at least he was someone, and he had stayed almost four times as long as anyone else. They were approaching being together for a year. She wanted to have something more, but felt she just couldn't expect it.

When she explored her home domain, Yoshiko began to see a pattern emerge. When she was a child, her father had abandoned and divorced her mother. Not long afterward he remarried and started a second family. She thinks she was about eight years old when she overheard him say to his new bride, "This time I'll get it right."

She did have her own room at her dad's new three-bedroom house. But the empty room was soon filled with cribs, and the cribs filled with toys and babies. Her dad was "getting it right." The time they spent together was less and less. One day at his house they were interrupted by one of her stepsiblings. Her dad excused himself and she turned on her computer. She spent more and more time online, as she could hear her dad playing with his young children elsewhere in the house.

Yoshiko began to feel her dad loved her stepsiblings more than her. That was twenty years ago. Here was a young woman, still under thirty, high up in her company echelon, who was still influenced by her home domain all those years ago. Somehow she saw herself as less-than, as a person who was never going to be good enough for a great guy, so she would settle for OK. She projected that sense of less-than, thinking that men saw her just like her dad seemed to: as nothing more than a person to be abandoned.

Yoshiko found herself in an unhappy relationship. She had become involved with a man who had little money, few employment prospects, and who depended on her for a place to live. She had settled for less in some ways because she was afraid she wasn't good enough to have a relationship with someone successful. A successful man was an independent man—who would be a threat to her, as he could leave her at any moment and finally "get it right."

Some people have such a deep-seated fear of being single that they're willing to settle for a partner who isn't exactly what they want to avoid being alone. A group out of the University of Toronto confirmed this in a study showing that the fear of being single predicts settling for less in a relationship. Being a member of a group, particularly a romantic dyad, has such importance that some people are willing to compromise a lot, even if it means dating, or marrying, a person they don't think is exactly the one for them.

OUTCAST AND CAST OUT

In some cases, alienation from our social world has become so embedded in popular culture that it becomes trivialized. All you have to do is watch how some kids use social media, tossing around rude and disrespectful language and attitudes for "comic" effect. Tweens and teens too young to understand the long-term repercussions of their behavior don't fully realize how seemingly small slights contribute to a greater problem of alienation in another person.

Recently, the media have made bullying a regular topic of focus and discussion. Yet even with the regular coverage, public perceptions of what bullying really means and does are still not fully accurate. In my work with adolescents, I've seen a great number of kids who were bullied, as well as the kids who are bullies themselves. What bullies actually seek to do is to alienate, not just bloody some other kid's nose.

Greg, for instance, was an angry teen. During elementary school, though, he was perceived as a leader of sorts. Athletic and charismatic, he had run a fiefdom on the playground. The kids he liked were part of the "cool" group. Be a friend to Greg and your school day went great. Those who didn't fit into his group were ignored. They wound up on the outskirts of the swing set and seesaws and often got a shove while waiting in the lunch line. While Greg never actually hit anyone, his posture underscored his intent. His words could be menacing and abrasive, just as if he had balled up his fist and knocked the wind out of your gut.

Greg was fourteen when he found himself in my office. He'd been a bully for one-third of his life. He loved it and had no intention of stopping. "I'm only here because of the court," he said.

Greg had also gotten into drugs and alcohol. When he was high, his bullying intensified, even to the point of physically injuring another student. Unwilling to get treatment, or even to see his drug use as a problem, Greg had pushed his parents to the limit. They eventually petitioned a judge, and Greg was sent to my program involuntarily.

Greg was good at being a bully. Even though he knew nothing about Theory of Mind, Greg knew how to use his influence to subordinate classmates he didn't like or approve of. With the exception of his circle, most classmates saw him as a bully. Yet he didn't see himself that way. And if he did, the image was very appealing. He didn't care about being respected; he just wanted to be feared.

By definition, bullying means unwanted and often aggressive behavior that involves a power imbalance. The key tool of the bully is intimidation. For intimidation to occur, one person—the victim or target—must be perceived as weaker than the other person—the bully. This relationship is repeated over and over, establishing the power hierarchy with the bully being "dominant" and the victim being "submissive." Bullies only physically harm targets once in a while; the means of intimidation are most often by spreading rumors, making threats, verbal attacks, and active exclusion of someone from the group. It's long been known that victims carry psychological scars, but we now know that they may carry physical scars too—on the brain. What the public needs to understand more fully is that this physiological insult can leave lasting damage at critical development points in the adolescent brain.

Martin Teicher, MD, a neuroscientist at Harvard Medical School, and his team have studied the effect of parental verbal abuse—a form of bullying—on kids' brains, showing that substantial psychological damage from verbal abuse is as severe as physical abuse. In a more recent study, he set out to look at how peer victimization might also affect the brain. By studying a group of 848 healthy young adults with no prior history of parental abuse or domestic violence exposure, the team found that indeed, peer verbal abuse, especially in the critical middle school years, did in fact lead to higher rates of anxiety, anger, depression, drug use, and other psychiatric conditions. That outcome is right on par with earlier findings on the effects of parental abuse. But when Dr. Teicher looked inside the brains of a subset of the volunteers who had reported varying incidences of bullying, he could clearly observe abnormalities in the same parts of the brain, the *corpus callosum*. This band of white brain matter connects the left and right sides of the brain so they can communicate with each other. In fact, people who are born without a corpus callosum have much greater difficulty recognizing the emotion in another person's face. Imagine the trouble this can cause in even the simplest interaction.

While the researchers have yet to learn how damage in this specific area will impact a person over the long term, the science indicates that peer abuse and alienation do in fact affect the physiology of the growing brain, altering brain structure and possibly reducing connectivity. It's as if the brain is only getting "half of the story," leading to difficulty interpreting the cues from the outside world and the people in it. What I find so utterly tragic about these findings is that other research indicates that the very victims of ostracism—the most frequent targets of bullies—may have a preexisting brain disadvantage, one that made them a prime target in the first place.

Understanding the importance of Theory of Mind in establishing healthy social relationships, British researchers at Queens College in London wanted to know whether or not a child's ToM might impact bullying behavior. Over a period of seven years, the researchers surveyed 2,232 children (and their families). They began by measuring each child's ToM at age five. Follow-up visits were made at age seven, ten, and twelve years old. The researchers discovered that children who scored lower on the ToM tasks at five were statistically more likely to be either victims or bully-victims (kids who became bullies themselves after being bullied). This study took into account all of the other family factors that could potentially influence the children's ToM and development of bullying tendencies.

So, having an inability to use ToM effectively makes a person more likely to be bullied. But why? Without these skills, a child has a harder time reading other children's social cues. Perhaps others find him slow: he doesn't get the jokes as quickly; he can't read the intent of others while they're playing. These kids are more likely to be perceived as "weird" or "odd," even if they're very intelligent but on a different developmental path with regard to social abilities. A person who can't read others well, and respond accordingly, will be more vulnerable to bullying. Ostracism via bullying can then further damage kids who've already been alienated.

As unfortunate as this turns out to be, it makes sense from a psychological point of view. We all expect the *other* person to wonder what we think or feel, even if we've never heard of ToM. When that doesn't happen, we can feel alienated, which makes us angry or afraid. So we respond, and not always in the best way. At this stage of development, "normal" children are still lacking the prefrontal cortex ability to moderate behavior. As a result, the response to others' odd behaviors is to separate, to cast out one who isn't perceived to fit, creating a vicious cycle of human behavior. And yet it's a cycle I believe we can change through anti-bullying educational programs and direct communication with our children about how to take another person's viewpoint.

But remember that Theory of Mind has two parts: how we think about others, and how they think about us. This makes the alienation of a less-aware child even more tragic. Even children with lower ToM ability can tell when they are being alienated. They just may have no clue why, unable to easily take another person's point of view.

————————— Exercise —————————

THE GROWING WALL

We can take steps with our kids to help break—or prevent—the alienation cycle we discussed. Kids with low Theory of Mind abilities, who are unable to connect, send alienating signals to other kids who don't "get them"; then the low ToM kids become targets, leading to further isolation. If you're a parent, then you already know how much kids love to be measured as they grow. In our house, we have what we call the "growing wall," marked with lines and dates so we can see how each child has grown inch by inch. But we can help our kids in the brain growth department as well, especially as it relates to their developing ToM. This goes for kids with lower ToM abilities, as well as other kids with higher ToM—help them build their empathy skills.

Next time you measure the kids add on some of these questions below. It doesn't matter how they respond, just opening up the discussion will help their minds develop. Give them a star for the answers that you can see light up in their extraordinary brains. And you, yourself, may also be very surprised at what you learn about your child:

- How did you show kindness today? And how did someone else show you kindness? How did that make you feel?
- You said you thought that Joey is "weird." Why do you think that?
- Do you think you might be weird to other kids? Does that matter?
- Do you think that all kids should be treated the same? Why?
- What about the weird or different kids? Should they be treated the same?
- Do you know what it feels like to be left out?

- What can you do tomorrow to help someone feel included?
- Did you know that sometimes just making eye contact and saying hi to kids who might feel left out can make a big difference in their day? Try it and come back and tell me how it made you feel.
- What were you most proud of today?

When asked questions like this, a child may at first say "I don't know." Don't take this as a conversation stopper. The child may fear giving a "wrong answer" and becoming diminished in your eyes. Whenever I hear children say "I don't know," I remind them this isn't school; I don't expect them to know, but I encourage them to wonder, to think about it, to take a chance and guess, because their answer is a reflection of their current maximum potential.

Pleasure in Pain

So, given the level of pain we cause when we exclude, why do we continue, after all these centuries, to inflict such psychic agony upon each other? One simple reason is that on a certain level, being a bully—that is, being "on top"—has the capacity to create pleasure. Whenever a behavior occurs with such frequency, it's reasonable to say that behavior has become reinforced. Reinforcement of a behavior usually entails some reward.

Bullies, it turns out, can score exceptionally high in Theory of Mind capabilities. British research shows that bullies actually outperformed their peers on social cognition tasks. In particular, among children aged seven to ten years, the "bullies" did a better job of identifying emotions and mental states of the main character in a story. It's uncanny how well bullies can pick just the right look, or the right words in the right tone, to let you know just how they feel about you. They can pick up masterfully on your emotional response, exploiting your fear to their own advantage. My patient Greg, who'd spent a third of his life being reinforced as a "leader," didn't want to give up bullying because the status felt good to him. He knew exactly what was going on. Without some growth in empathy and moral reasoning abilities, it was my guess that he'd grow into an adult who didn't care if he was liked as long as he got to stay on top. He'd continue to be interested in what other people thought and felt about him, as a person to be feared, without considering what the other person's fear felt like.

This pleasure experienced by bullies helps explain the remarkable level of bullying that goes on among adolescents, not just in our society, but every society ever studied. Canadian researchers at Brock University have estimated annual prevalence rates of bullying among adolescents worldwide at 10 to 60 percent: admittedly a wide range. But when you put that in real, worldwide numbers, you're looking at somewhere between one hundred million to six hundred million adolescents directly involved in bullying each year.

But the pleasure that is seemingly derived from someone else's misfortune—especially when that person isn't in our group—may also contribute to cruelty. Human beings, it would appear, are wired with the capacity to feel too good when another feels bad, especially when that person is somehow in competition with us. Brain imaging scans reveal that when someone we see as an "other" endures pain or misfortune, the brain's reward center becomes active, releasing a dose of pleasure and satisfaction that is comparable to eating a good meal.

For an everyday example, think about the guy who is beside himself with glee as a friend rolls on the ground in agony after being hit in the testicles, or the amusement many people find in watching videos of skateboard accidents. Where's the humor in *The Three Stooges?* It's in the harmful slapstick. Now I'm not judging you here, perhaps you laugh out loud at Curly, Larry, and Moe. There's even a television program on National Geographic TV called *The Science of Stupid,* which tells stories about the many ways people injure and embarrass themselves. The show's producers perhaps feel legitimate in celebrating painful accidents by explaining how science failed the unfortunate souls, many of whom wind up in the hospital.

The degree to which we feel sadistic pleasure depends on a person's degree of empathy, but we all have this neural wiring in place. If natural empathy is lacking or if group hostility is encouraged in the culture, bullying can become downright pleasurable. And since humans will always gravitate toward pleasurable feelings, social psychology will always degenerate toward bullying when those particular cultural attitudes are in place.

But why are we wired this way? And how can we use ToM to override our innate tendencies?

TEND AND DEFEND: ENGINEERED FOR OUT-GROUPING

The New South Wales Cricket Association was hosting the visiting English cricket team. The clubs were international rivals, and the home team fans had packed the stadium. The English players were trouncing their hosts. But the Australian fans were unperturbed as their star batsman, Billy Murdoch, approached the wicket. But soon into his at-bat, the umpire, a British Victorian hired by the English team, called Murdoch out. Two thousand fans erupted, invading the field and assaulting the English players. The year was 1879, and the incident became known as the Sydney Riot.

A hundred years later, at Madison Square Garden in 1979, the visiting Boston Bruins were in a hockey battle with their rival New York Rangers. Hockey is known for its "sanctioned" violence, with players routinely taking shots at each other, pushing each other around on the ice. In one of these on-ice battles, a Rangers fan cut a Bruin's face when he hit him with a rolled-up program, then stole his hockey stick. Terry O'Reilly, a Boston Bruin, jumped into the stands to run after the attacker, followed by several other Bruins. A violent melee broke out between the fans and players. Forever enshrined on video, one of the players was caught on camera taking the shoe of a Rangers fan and mercilessly beating him with it.

Sports events stir fans' passion for their teams. As the clock ticks during a game, the surge and power of a collective desire to win becomes palpable. The opponent becomes, momentarily, the enemy. This group, now a perfect example of spontaneous cooperation with a shared belief, can easily turn into a mob. So it is through our human ability to cooperate that we can sometimes find ourselves in the midst of scary and disturbing events. Scientific studies show that individuals who feel part of a collective are more likely to engage in "all-out war." They're more willing to spend their resources for the good of the group—if the general goal is to destroy a competing faction. But you don't need science to prove mob behavior, especially if you simply observe certain individuals at professional sports events. Is this really the best that a group of humans can do?

From a neuro-evolutionary perspective, the answer appears to be yes. According to research led by Professor C. K. De Dreu from the University of Amsterdam, our neurohormone oxytocin—the "cuddle" hormone we discussed earlier—plays a strong role in this grouping phenomenon in three critical ways. First, the presence of oxytocin release in our brains enables us to place people into categories such as in and out groups. Second, it dampens the fear response in the limbic system, which opens the way for more trust. And third, it increases empathy and concern in the prefrontal cortex—but specifically for the group with whom we're in a cooperative relationship.

This evolutionary adaptation of our grouping mechanisms explains the Sydney Riots of 1879, the Bruins attack of 1979, every war in history, the current race riots around the world, and the nationalism, racism, and bigotry we experience on a daily basis. This is the dark side of oxytocin: we will favor members of our in-group over members of an out-group. This favoritism leads to greater cooperation among group members at the expense of out-group members.

Our strong, empathic, and caring bond—so critical for human survival for centuries—also creates the framework for *not* cooperating with and defending against threatening outsiders. Oxytocin is not just involved in reproduction and staying with a partner but, as De Dreu's study explains, oxytocin leads to a "tend-and-defend" behavior within a group. Unlike vasopressin, which can prompt aggression, oxytocin enhances a coming together to protect one's group against invaders. But still, it creates an "us-versus-them" mentality that makes cooperation between groups very, very challenging.

As part of a group, you may be surrounded by complete strangers and yet find ways to cooperate because of your shared values and beliefs. This type of cooperation can make a huge difference in people's lives, as assorted group memberships provide them with routes to connection, new friends, activities, and resources. But on the flip side, when the group is threatened or mobilized in some way, humans have a way of reinforcing the group by punishing those who don't follow the rules and rewarding those who do, enforcing group loyalty in the context of shared values and goals. Pushed beyond cooperation into subservience, the individual may lose his or her own moral equilibrium. The expression used by dictators, military leaders, and even some elected officials, "You're either with us or against us," pretty well sums up this phenomenon. And it is Theory of Mind that lets you say with sincerity, even after the most heinous war crime, that "I was only following orders."

> ▶ **LYING FOR LOYALTY**
>
> Sometimes we can be so loyal to our group that we are willing to lie to protect it. Lying to protect one's group can start young, and it actually increases as one gets older. In fact, an eleven-year-old child is more likely to tell a lie to protect his or her group than a seven- or nine-year-old.
>
> If you think about it, lying out of loyalty is a completely normal and even forgivable human behavior. It's what most of us do for our friends and expect them to do for us without any advance contract to do so. Haven't you ever lied to protect a friend? Maybe as a teen, you told a friend's mom he was at your house when in reality he'd sneaked out to meet his girlfriend. Or at work, have you covered for a fellow employee who was late or taking a long lunch? Ironically, the more trust and oxytocin you have in a relationship, the more likely you are to lie to protect that person. And also, when the group bond is broken by a member, that person becomes a traitor. On a high enough level, that's still a highly punishable crime in most countries, one that carries the death penalty in many.
>
> In my teen treatment program, patients tell me about the lies they've told to protect their friends. Their motivation is concern, and not just the threatening credo "snitches get stitches." In fact, if someone else tells on their friend, they may get angry and even threatening.

Once you're on the outside of this kind of cooperative group, you're at a much higher risk of alienation because you're now an "outsider" and your value to that in-group as a human being is greatly diminished. Scientists from Princeton University have distinguished several types of groups that are commonly dehumanized. First are those judged low on perceived warmth, trustworthiness, and competence; they may also tend to elicit disgust and avoidance. From my experience, a lot of people with addiction and psychiatric conditions are dumped into this category. Racists, bigots, homophobes, and others dump their targets into this category with chilling results. Next, groups deemed competent but untrustworthy are more likely to elicit *Schadenfreude*, a delight at another person's misfortune: the trials and tribulations of movie stars, politicians, the unreachably rich, and famous athletes represent this group alienated by others. The third most commonly devalued group encompasses those who are pitied. They may be likable but they are not competent. How many of our senior citizens, especially people with dementias, fall into this category?

When an entire group perceives itself as vulnerable, very dangerous things can happen. In 2014 and 2015, the United States was rocked by protests and riots of outrage following several highly publicized cases in which white police officers killed unarmed African American men. When a person belonging to a group feels another member has suffered prejudice, there is a great chance that the collective group will rise up against the perceived outgroup that caused the injustice. Faculty from New York University explored this with college students and their identification with their college. The researchers found that "among people who are highly identified with a group, learning about the group's injustice leads to short-term increases in group-serving behavior." This can lead to all kinds of outcomes, from an increased ability to raise funds on the group's behalf to getting volunteers signed up for action.

Those members who cooperate in times of war may risk their lives for the promise of some reward. In fact, the greater the potential reward, the greater risk a group member is willing to take. This is another dark side of Theory of Mind, as charismatic leaders may exploit an individual group member. When we use ToM to distort the intention of another person or group, human beings can commit chilling atrocities, as we know all too well.

▶ **JUST SAY HELLO**

Alienation and subsequent loneliness have a new enemy with one of America's most influential women, Oprah Winfrey, who in 2014 kicked off a campaign called "Just Say Hello." With the partnership of CNN's Sanjay Gupta and Skype, as well as the help of numerous celebrities, videos, and a Twitter campaign (#justsayhello), Oprah has set out to tackle what has been called an epidemic of loneliness. Announcing the campaign on Piers Morgan's CNN television program, Oprah opened a dialogue about our mutual need for validation:

> I started to see that pattern. And what I realized is that everybody is looking for the same thing. No matter if it's politicians, senators, presidents, Beyoncé in all of her Beyoncé-ness. We're all looking to know, "Did you see me, did you hear me, and did what I say mean anything to you?" So just saying hello is a way of validating even a stranger.

Oprah may not have known at the time that she was speaking directly about the power and influence we have with Theory of Mind.

ALIENATION TO ALLIANCE

Here's something I want you to think about: whenever you think more about yourself than other people, you're at risk of alienating someone. Whenever we feel that someone is thinking more of him- or herself than others, especially us, we too can feel alienated. You know and I know that it feels awful to be on the receiving end of rejection. You now understand how we as a larger, human group have evolved to create, maintain, and protect our subgroups—for survival. In many parts of the world, the need to do this still exists. But in the developed world, we have the opportunity to learn from our past and move into the future. Yes, these are big thoughts, yet they start on a fundamental, day-to-day level. Take the story of Jane.

A mid-level manager who constantly put in extra hours without ever being asked, Jane was well respected by those under her and those above her in the organization. She came in to see me one day to talk about her work. A corporate restructuring was going on, and everyone was on edge. Jane felt that some of her co-workers were backstabbing her, trying to climb over her to ensure their job security. She began to hate going to work. Her boss noticed a change in attitude. Concerned, she asked Jane to stop by for a chat. "She asked me what was going on," Jane told me. "I had always seemed so enthusiastic at work, and now she was getting concerned that I may be looking for a different job given the upcoming restructuring."

Jane was lucky to have a good boss who liked her and noticed a change. Without meaning to, Jane's boss had caused all her employees to feel less-than and at risk of losing their job. Jane responded with anxiety and mistrust, which led her to dread going into work where she felt unsafe. This got her boss's attention. If they hadn't talked, Jane would probably have been let go, as her boss had noticed that Jane's productivity and apparent loyalty had decreased. Jane and her boss had both alienated each other and placed themselves at risk of losing an alliance.

We alienate ourselves from other people all the time. We influence the way they begin to see us. If we present ourselves in a way that turns someone else off, that person probably won't want to form an alliance, but instead get as far away from us as possible. We've all been around people like that as well. Something about the way they act makes us not want to be with them. Sometimes they're arrogant and boastful. People like this make us worry that a relationship with them will be lopsided, with them taking more and giving less. Other people appear too insecure. This risks more lopsided relationships: we're holding their hand and encouraging them more than they would do for us. Sometimes we shy away from a romantic relationship in which the other person seems too in love too soon. We worry that person may become possessive, restrictive, and isolate us from other relationships.

Sad to say, we may be doing things as well that alienate other people from us. If we really do control no one but influence everyone, then it has to happen. We can just as easily make other people dislike us and see us as less-than, as we can influence them to like us and want to create an alliance.

From an I-M perspective, whether we're practicing alienation or building alliances, we're doing the best that we can do at that moment in time. The question is, why would any of us behave in such a way as to jeopardize any alliance at all? On some level, we must still think and feel it is still the best we can do.

▶ **I-M IMPACT: REFRAME YOUR SELF-ESTEEM**

As low as our self-esteem may sometimes dive, it's important to remember that we're simply at an I-M—our maximum potential at any given moment. As we recognize that we're doing the best we can, we can reflect on whether this low self-esteem is something we like or condone in ourselves. The feeling may be familiar, but is it comfortable? If you don't like it, you can change it.

Rather than blame something in our home or social domain, we can choose to hold ourselves responsible for having low self-esteem. This may seem like a big ask, especially when the chips are down, but think about it. Taking responsibility in and of itself is empowering, and so is moving yourself from feeling "less-than-I-can" to the "best-that-I-can."

With the I-M Approach, you have the ability to increase your own self-esteem, which ultimately makes you a more attractive member of a group.

This is where the I-M becomes a road map to insight. If our self-esteem is low, what might our other domains have to do with it? Is our Ic domain insecure, and does our biological domain respond with fear? Fear is designed to make us run away. At a job interview, do we unconsciously get so nervous that we present ourselves in such a way that no boss would hire us? Although it seems that this would *not* be the best we could do, if fear is driving our I-M, then we've actually done perfectly: we haven't been hired, and we've avoided what our fear led us to perceive as a potentially dangerous situation. Sometimes we perpetuate a "less-than" image. Many of my patients with insecurity expect to be rejected. Over and over they may "shoot themselves in the foot" in a relationship. Unconsciously they influence and hasten the very rejection they so dread, but by doing so retain some semblance of control of that social snub. How have you contributed to being alienated by someone else? Low self-esteem can have an enormous impact, yet it still results in the best that a person with low self-esteem can do.

In the final chapter, we'll take a look at how we can fine-tune our Theory of Mind to make it more likely that people will really "get" us.

5

Nature

OUR INNATE CAPACITY FOR CHOOSING CONNECTION

The more one judges, the less one loves.
—Honoré de Balzac, *Physiologie Du Mariage*

You've been learning about Theory of Mind and how human nature works with regard to how we perceive each other and accept or reject each other. Including some people and excluding others are both in our nature. But you now know how we influence "human nature" through Theory of Mind (ToM), by taking another's viewpoint and responding accordingly. A dark side to this capability is in all of us: when we use it to put other people down and alienate them. In all of us there is also a vulnerability: we might be a target of that dark side when someone else makes us feel devalued. Yet in all of us, too, is the ability to make others feel the best-that-they-can-be, increasing their sense of value. Both of these choices are in our nature.

In this chapter, we'll explore why we make one choice or the other—why we go to the dark side at all, choosing to alienate and not align with others. How we make these choices will influence how people really "get" us. As social animals we want to be in a group where people understand us—they get us. We want them to want us; we want to be a part of the group. The last place we want to be is on the outside. When we use ToM to make a connection, we are satisfying one of our basic human needs, one that cannot be ignored. In this chapter, we'll also explore how we can use ToM to influence our admittance into a group, and how to connect, making more allies in the process. Let's take a look at how this works.

In desperation Sheila had cut into her forearm, superficially at first, but then deep enough to buy her a trip to the emergency room. The doctors there didn't treat her with care and compassion, but with disgust. After all, her wounds were self-inflicted.

Now in my office, Sheila showed me the myriad scars, so carelessly tended to in the ER that her arms looked like Frankenstein's monster's. Wounds that could easily have been sutured, minimizing the chance of scarring, had instead been closed using a staple gun—apparently by angry, dismissive doctors wanting to spend as little time as possible with this "annoying" patient. Their attitude toward Sheila added insult to injury. The staff dismissed her, confirming her worst nightmare: that she was indeed a worthless, less-than-human person who deserved to be cast out.

Sheila was a smart, musically talented, attractive teenager with unlimited potential who had been abused, bullied, and molested in her early years. Cutting was her desperate attempt at masking a deep and profound psychic pain with physical pain. But rather than treating Sheila with compassion, working with her to understand what prompted the cutting, the ER doctors perceived her only as "a cutter," further undermining her self-esteem. And from Sheila's perspective, these were *doctors* who treated her that way, professionals, so they must be right: hers was a useless body that deserved to be cut up.

To these very busy and no doubt tired and overburdened ER doctors, here was a perfectly healthy person creating unnecessary injuries, which they then had to manage. From a ToM perspective, the doctors felt devalued by having to waste their skills and time. To them, this was not a child who'd been hit by a car, or someone who got unlucky with a chainsaw, or somebody having a massive coronary. Here was a young "basket case" taking up their valuable time. But they didn't have to say a word to convey how they perceived her. Every staple was an ER physician screaming, *You cut yourself, so why should I really care about you? I have better things to do than take care of someone who can't take care of herself.* Without realizing it, the medical team had recreated Sheila's childhood experience of being demeaned, rejected, and alienated, leaving her to feel more and more isolated and alone. The message registered clear as day to Sheila.

Sheila's story shows the power we have over each other through Theory of Mind. It gives us the capacity to exclude or include. Both of these choices are in our nature. If you are interested in what I think about you (and you know by now that you definitely are: it's human nature, the heart of ToM, to need to know what others think of us), then I have an opportunity to make you feel really, really bad: to increase your anxiety, your anger, and your sadness. I can influence you to feel like a worthless piece of garbage as easily as I can influence you to feel like a worthwhile, interesting person. Other people can influence me in the very same way. But by understanding ToM, and putting it to work, expressing the dark side of our nature no longer always has to be a given. We can learn to actively select our better nature of trust and alliance, the side of human nature that pulls us forward to a more productive I-Maximum (I-M): the view that at any moment, we are doing the best we can in the given circumstances.

▶ I-M IMPACT: CLASH OF THE I-MS

Let's look more deeply at the I-Ms of the two parties in the story of my patient Sheila and the ER doctors. Sheila's low self-image was perpetuated by the dismissive and disgusted response of the ER physicians and nurses. In her mind, she became the Frankenstein she was seen as by the dismissive doctors. What could she have done in that moment to prevent further injury to her self-image? How could she have protected her Ic domain—how she sees herself through the eyes of others? How could Sheila have turned things around in her own mind? Perhaps by applying ToM herself to see how exhausted the doctors were in that moment. A busy night in the ER means long hours, no rest or food, and a lot of tragedy and trauma. Doctors are humans, too, and they have the enormous responsibility of saving lives, often with precious minutes ticking away. In a less hectic environment, Sheila would probably have received more empathy and more careful treatment. In their eyes, Sheila put herself there, needlessly taking their time for patients whom they thought *really* needed their help.

Had the doctors used more ToM, they might have slowed down to take in Sheila's whole picture. She was like anyone who needed medical attention. Without the ER trip, she might have bled to death. Though the injury was self-inflicted, it was a symptom of a serious condition, just one they didn't have the expertise to deal with. They needed to remember that all patients require compassion, not just staples and stitches. Psychiatric conditions are no less important or worthy of healing than any others. Every patient is a person who has value.

Even though I believe that we are all operating at a certain I-M, the best we can do in that moment, remember this: we can change that I-M through choices we make in response to our circumstances.

Look at your own past. Think of a time when you felt alienated from someone. The other person was devaluing you, and your limbic system responded, perhaps getting angry, fearful, or sad. But now shift to the prefrontal cortex and use your Theory of Mind to take *the other person's* perspective. The best they could do was alienate. What was going on in their domains that made this their choice? How do you see the other person's perspective differently? How would you change the way they saw the situation for you to get the outcome you wanted? Even small changes can have big effects.

OUR DARK SIDE REVEALED: IT AIN'T PRETTY

To fully understand our own role in alienating others, we need to make a deep dive into our dark side. We all have the same human needs, desires, hungers, and dreams. In our evolutionary history, we came from a wild place full of struggle, and we have emerged as a more or less civilized species—although considering the destructive behaviors that prevail among both individuals and nations on the planet, we still have a long way to go.

And, as you'll recall from the first chapter, we are and will always be influenced by brain chemicals such as oxytocin and vasopressin that make our brains tick and affect all our decisions.

In chapter 4 we looked at alienation and how, with the help of vasopressin, we can derive pleasure from being disrespectful, mean, or even abusive or violent toward someone, especially if the person is in an out-group and we perceive ourselves to be protecting our in-group. But it's extremely hard to see sometimes that each of us continues to do this in many ways, small and large, especially in our modern world where our groups aren't so clearly defined as "in" or "out." Instead, they intersect like so many circuits on a silicon chip.

We find it convenient to lie to ourselves and say, "But I'm not like that guy—I don't enjoy putting other people down." With our ToM at work, we don't want others to see us that way because by revealing our darker nature we could be perceived as less valuable. The tirades of drunken celebrities, and the provocative "hate speech" so prevalent in the news and social media, only serve to show, despite this denial, how easily any of us can publicly display our dark side. Until we can be honest about our human shortcomings in this regard, we can't begin to change, and we'll continue to repeat harmful behaviors toward one another.

At first, many of us refuse to admit that we could take pleasure in someone else's misfortune, that we could purposefully demean, degrade, and disrespect that person to feel good ourselves. We don't want to be seen in a way that might diminish our value to our family, social group, or community. But the courage it takes to look at our own darker side can eventually leave us stronger, wiser, and significantly more valuable in our own eyes and in the eyes of others. Just as lying, when exposed, is perceived as a liability, honesty is generally regarded as an asset. Honesty is perhaps the highest virtue, and virtuous people are prized members of most groups—at least of the groups most of us are drawn to, we hope.

So let's get honest about the two key areas in which improving our Theory of Mind could help us: our darker feelings toward others, and our negative feelings about ourselves.

The Fleeting Rewards of the Dark Side

You might have seen the photograph on the Internet of a young Helen Keller cuddling a little dog, captioned "Helen Keller and her beloved cat, Mittens." This image apparently made a lot of people laugh because it was shared millions of times through social media. Would it make you laugh to think that Helen Keller thought a dog was a cat? Most of us would be hard-pressed to admit we would laugh at a joke made at the expense of a blind person.

And yet, as we discussed in the last chapter, there's a part of our brains that gets rewarded when we define ourselves as a member of a more desirable group—people with sight in this case—at someone else's expense. We are wired this way. And in a situation such as the photo sharing, even if you think you're just joking and not actually making fun of someone else's misfortune, that other person may not take it as a joke and can feel alienated.

But for some people, and perhaps for all of us at some time, the pleasure of excluding someone just feels good, even if momentarily. In fact, one reason for our impulse to exclude others is that it does, on some level, feel good. The impulse may be traceable to our primitive survival instinct: when resources like food and shelter were scarce, denying some people access to those resources meant having more for ourselves. We still take pleasure in the feeling of safety in protecting ourselves and our group—and our brains will always gravitate to pleasure-enhancing experiences. We can't seem to help ourselves, even when we know—using our more recently developed higher brains, the prefrontal cortex— that to include others in our group will likely be more beneficial in the long run, expanding our network and our resources.

But on some other level we know that excluding behaviors like putting someone down, lying, or cheating is not the right thing to do. Still, if alienating someone is pleasurable at such a primitive level, like any pleasurable experience, it can become habit-forming, even addictive. It's hard to resist seeking the reward that comes with the spike of dopamine elicited by these behaviors. The neurohormone that helps control the brain's reward and pleasure center, dopamine is also behind the high induced by alcohol and other drugs and from overeating, gambling, and other compulsive behaviors. The dopamine signal promises a real reward from the behavior itself, though with addiction the signal itself, the surge of pleasure, *becomes* the reward, tricking us into repeating the behavior over and over, even if it is contrary to our values and detrimental to our health and sense of worth. Could it be that any pleasure-seeking habit, including alienating people to protect our group, could have a similar effect?

Cheating

One way that people frequently succeed in alienating others is by cheating. But if the risk of getting caught were lowered, then would more people do it, despite its effect on others? That was the question posed by Swiss researchers at the University of Basel recently. In their study, the team gave some subjects doses of dopamine and others a placebo, but no one knew which they had received. Then they played an economic bargaining game. The game could be played in two modes, one in which unfair behavior could be punished, and one in which it could not.

What did the researchers observe? The people who were given extra dopamine were indeed more likely to cheat if they knew they weren't going to get caught or suffer any consequences. The dopamine infusion appeared to increase the subjects' pleasure in getting away with cheating. But when a punishment was involved, the dopamine had no effect. The researchers concluded, "Even a single dose of dopamine may bring selfish behavior to the fore."

So even as we see how these biological mechanisms play an important role in our behavior, we do not have to be slaves to them. Your Theory of Mind reminds you when you're doing something that will serve to only exclude or alienate someone. Most of us are keenly aware of these behaviors. And, while at some level we feel "good" when we hurt others to protect ourselves and our group, at another level we feel a negative feeling, guilt, because our ToM tells us what it would feel like to be excluded. So we must make a choice in those moments to take the high road, to keep in check those comments and behaviors that may provide only fleeting pleasure and reward. Instead, we can choose to enhance our I-M potential and engage in those positive behaviors and responses that offer the lasting benefits of real connection.

▶ **A NEUROHORMONE FOR THE LONG GAME**

Remy was what I called a "roller coaster kid." Even as a youngster he took more chances doing jumps with his BMX bike than the other kids did. The only child of two full-time working parents, he sought out thrills into his teen years, always looking for that dopamine rush. Dopamine, and adrenaline, became a need for Remy, and only a new thrill would give him the jolt of those neurohormones. Without the thrills brought on by risk taking behaviors, he felt bored and empty. He had no close attachments with others, no best friend or group of regular buddies, and he spent large amounts of time by himself, an indicator that perhaps he had low levels of oxytocin. But when the nearby lake froze each winter, he could hardly wait to get out there for a stunt that to him was pure heaven: a midnight car spin on the ice.

This type of imbalance led Remy into drug use, then into serious drug abuse and addiction. His need for dopamine grew and grew, until no amount of the drugs he consumed could sate his craving and he finally overdosed. He survived, and a year later, with treatment that included establishing new relationships with a variety of people (his social domain) and rebuilding his relationship with his parents (his home domain), he was able to fulfill his basic need for connection that had been buried for years. Remy now felt the power of oxytocin, the neurohormone of trust. Oxytocin doesn't come at you like dopamine; rather, it's the warm hum of acceptance and belonging that has the lasting value dopamine can only pretend to provide.

THE HONEST SELF

We all know facts about ourselves we might not want other people to know: mistakes we made in our past—or mistakes others have made, such as abusing or neglecting us as children—that have left us with the feeling we were unwanted and had no value. We often try to relegate these secrets to a memory chest buried at the bottom of the sea of our unconscious, not wanting to face these parts of ourselves, denying ourselves the opportunity to reassess, or learn from them even years later.

From a Theory of Mind perspective, the reason we do this is clear. A secret is not a secret because of what I have done. A secret is a secret because I worry, *Will you see me differently if you know my secret?* I wonder, *Could I be devalued by you?* which would leave me feeling alienated and at risk. That's why we resist looking at ourselves honestly, which in turn keeps our true selves hidden both from ourselves and from others. We may not like what we find. And we may not trust that you'll like what you find in me if you really "get me."

The I-M Approach can help us overcome that resistance by allowing us to stop judging ourselves. Remember, when you see yourself at an I-M, you're seeing a snapshot of yourself at your current maximum potential doing the best you can in that moment. When the circumstances in your life change, your I-M changes. Resistance to change and avoiding the possibility of new insights is itself a new I-M, one that typically indicates that you're worried or fearful.

Excessive worry about a challenge is an extension of the stress response: fight, flight, or freeze. This often causes us to delay or avoid dealing with the problem, which is basically a flight response. We run because we don't believe we're strong enough to withstand the threat, and we risk being devalued in other people's perceptions. But when we look at our response through the lens of the I-M Approach, we can see that we don't have to immediately condemn ourselves or assume that others will. We can, instead, choose to simply look at everything in our past as a series of I-Ms: at any given time we were doing the best we could under those circumstances.

Ironically, it's by running from our problems and our past that we actually *do* undermine ourselves, convincing ourselves that we don't have the inner strength to confront whatever we thought was the initial threat. We don't even give ourselves a chance to learn something new that might change our I-M. By seeing and accepting ourselves (and others) at our current maximum with the potential to achieve a new maximum with new knowledge and circumstances, we are enabled to feel less weak and vulnerable. We can discover that worrying about what other people will think doesn't protect us; it actually prevents us from realizing our best potential maximum. We can ask ourselves: *What's going on in my four life domains? What small changes might influence the things and people in my two external domains (home and social)? What might positively influence my two internal domains (biological and Ic)?*

Take the story of Amy, age twenty-five, who clearly recalls the day twenty years ago when she was at her friend Claire's birthday party. Someone was in the bathroom when Amy needed to go, and she could no longer hold it. Her subsequent "accident" caused her great embarrassment. In a five-year-old's brain, ToM is firmly in place. Amy remembered the other children making fun of her, calling her a baby. She felt horrified, humiliated, alienated from the other kids, and she cried for her mom to take her home.

That early experience would be triggered later in Amy's life at various social events, manifesting itself as an anxiety attack. The initial experience had been buried for so long that it didn't register as a memory until Amy finally dug it up during therapy. The stress and anxiety that various social functions triggered caused Amy to retreat, excluding herself before she could be excluded by others. That one childhood experience led to a crippling of Amy's self-esteem as she grew into adulthood.

Low self-esteem often stems from the unpleasant experience of feeling devalued at some time in our lives. It's easy to see why we wouldn't want to consciously stir up a feeling like that, so, out of fear and shame, we erect a wall to keep that memory and the associated feeling out of our conscious thoughts. It's a perfectly reasonable I-M response, that is, until we become dissatisfied with remaining frozen in an I-M that locks us in the past.

Having linked this past incident with her current social anxiety, Amy realized that she was no longer at her five-year-old I-M. She came to see herself as a bright college graduate with the world as her oyster. She can now safely look back at that childhood birthday party and examine just how those feelings could still trigger her fear response in social settings. She gained insight into her current I-M and how to use Theory of Mind to accurately assess other people's perception of her as an adult. She feels accepted and included today. She is not a five-year-old girl having "accidents" anymore.

Our brain is at a different I-M in every moment of our lives. We can develop a more appropriate response to our current challenges, one that breaks through fear and allows us to experience the trust that comes from feeling respected and valued. We find then that trust is the antidote to fear.

——————— Exercise ———————

UNDERSTANDING WHAT YOU FEEL

Consider a time when you felt angry, anxious, or sad. Perhaps you felt that way because you perceived someone sending you a signal that you were less-than, leaving you at higher risk of shifting from a sense of inclusion to alienation. Truly understanding *why* you feel what you feel creates an advantage for you, an opportunity to respond less impulsively and more thoughtfully. Happy or sad, courageous or scared, peaceful or angry: the first step in using these feelings to your advantage is to recognize that you have them. That's a function of your prefrontal cortex, the brain's executive center. What you think affects what you feel, and what you feel then affects the actions you may take. Let's take a look at some ways this might play out with some common feelings—anger, fear, and sadness—in negotiating our inclusion in a group.

Anger—An angry feeling implies you want a situation to change and are preparing to activate the "fight" branch of your limbic flight-fight-freeze response. Do you feel that someone's threatening to kick you out of a group? Does your anger serve to shoehorn yourself back in by making the threatening person leave or get kicked out himself?

Fear—A scared feeling implies you don't see yourself as strong enough to fight. So the "flight" branch activates, urging you to get away from the situation and hope the danger passes—possibly still leaving you a part of the group but with a diminished stature in the hierarchy.

Sadness—A sad feeling freezes you. Not strong enough to fight and unable to get away, you opt for inertia. Your limbic brain suggests you become so invisible that the group won't even know you're there. But you pay a price: invisibility limits your access to the survival enhancement of full membership.

Once you know why you're feeling what you're feeling, you can respond using your prefrontal cortex instead of responding emotionally and reflexively. By shifting your unconscious concern of being alienated into consciousness, you have many more choices, anticipating the consequence of each option.

THE POWER OF THE BENEFACTOR

Self-esteem is a term that really needs to be untangled. It gets thrown around in popular psychology and self-help settings without proper definition. One must have high self-esteem; one must build it; our kids must get lots of it; one feels awful when self-esteem is low, and so on. But what does it really mean, and why does it seem to matter so much?

The National Association for Self-Esteem (yes, there is one!) defines self-esteem as "the experience of being capable of meeting life's challenges and being worthy of happiness." Self-esteem is not something that comes and goes every day like a good or bad mood. Rather, it's a mind-set about oneself that reflects one's sense of competence and worth—two things that aren't inborn but come with life experiences. Does one feel capable of responding to one's own and others' performance expectations, whether personal, professional, or societal? Does one feel a basic sense of worth, of value and importance to oneself and others—not necessarily dependent on their competency? Competence and worth are both qualities that you can influence in yourself and others with Theory of Mind.

Our self-esteem is directly linked to what we think others think of us. We all, to some degree, tie our self-esteem to our perception of our value in other people's eyes. The fact that this is reciprocal, that it works both ways, is the true power of ToM. At every moment we have an opportunity to remind others of their value, and when we do this, we enhance our own value. We can expand our protective group; we can make nurturing other people's self-esteem a priority in all our relationships, which enhances everyone's life. Studies show that people with healthy self-esteem are better at regulating their emotions when under stressful situations. As we've seen, we regulate our emotions in the prefrontal cortex. In fact, those with low self-esteem appear to have less brain volume in some of these brain areas. Additionally, the healthier your self-esteem is, the less likely you are to perceive criticism. Psychologists from Dartmouth College showed in a recent study that people with low self-esteem perpetuate a lower self-image by being hypersensitive to criticism.

Healthy self-esteem not only helps us feel safer, it means we have an opportunity to make someone else feel safer too. And when we help someone else feel safer we increase our value to them, making us a greater resource to the group—kind of a "value boomerang effect." I call this phenomenon the *power of the benefactor.*

Here's an everyday example. One day as I entered the Boston subway system, I watched as the woman in front of me tried to swipe her subway card. She couldn't get it to work. Her family members, who seemed to be foreign tourists, were already through the gate and were waving their arms, encouraging her. As she tried again, I could see that the card didn't have enough value on it. I tapped her shoulder and swiped my own card, letting her go through. After I passed through myself, the woman's family members were reaching for their wallets and acting as if I'd saved her life. I just smiled, waved their offer away, and told them to have a great time as I walked on. The entire exchange took seconds and was completely spontaneous. The resulting message to the family? A nice American in a large city valued them enough to help them. But the boomerang of value came right back around to me as a benefactor. Being a benefactor feels great, and it connects me to people, even people I'll never see again, and often (as in this case) at a tiny cost to myself.

Being a benefactor helps us capitalize on our need to be valued by letting others know that we see *them* as valuable. If they, in turn, see *us* as more valuable, we've become a more highly prized and contributing member of the group, whether just as a dyad—benefactor and beneficiary—or within a larger group. There's no more effective way to mutually enhance self-esteem than using ToM to connect with other people at this level.

▶ **CALLING ALL BENEFACTORS**

When you hang around generous and giving people, your companions likely have both a highly developed ToM and high self-esteem. So where do you find these people? One of the most common places is volunteer organizations. Here's where people congregate to give of themselves to a cause that's meaningful to society. These are a group of benefactors, all using ToM to make the world, or their niche in it, a better place. The odds of meeting someone here who "gets" you, who values you, are probably higher than average.

Opportunities to volunteer are endless, as the need is always there. Whether it's the March of Dimes, Boys and Girls Clubs, scouting, libraries, recycling groups, volunteer teaching or tutoring, art projects, neighborhood spruce-up days, or any of the thousands of nonprofits and community organizations out there, the possibilities are unlimited. Giving of yourself is called altruism, and altruism feels good. Why? From a ToM point of view, someone else sees you as caring. People seen as caring are admired and respected. Respect leads to value, and value leads to trust, trust leads to membership, which boosts self-esteem. As I said, the possibilities are endless.

WHEN THEORY OF MIND BREAKS DOWN

As much as we may sometimes try to reach people through ToM, there are times when it doesn't work well, or at all. It can and does break down for us and for others for various reasons. Sometimes we "turn off" our ToM capacity without realizing it, often by turning off our attention to the people we encounter day to day altogether, e.g., stereotyping people because of their race, pigeonholing people because of how they look, or because of their role or job (clerk, politician, boss, etc.). Many people are so focused on handheld electronic devices that they pretty much ignore everything and everyone around them—even the people who want to connect with them the most. Sometimes, though, ToM is turned off because our biological domain has an I-M in which ToM is not as functional to start with, as in autism.

In the case of autism, neuroscientists have identified a problem with interference with the mirror neurons we talked about in chapter 1, causing ToM deficits. In a recent study from the University of Tokyo, researchers worked with twenty-five autistic teenagers between the ages of eleven and eighteen. These teens were found to have what appears to be an *over*-connectivity between the mirror neuron system and the ToM system. While at first this seems counterintuitive, the over-connectivity suggests that the system is working overly hard, trying to compensate for immaturity or a difficulty in development. The increased cross-talk between the two systems leaves the person with autism functionally impaired at reading ToM in others, as well as using it themselves.

One striking characteristic of people on the autism spectrum is their discomfort in making eye contact. Ami Klin, who wrote the foreword to this book, has discovered that a decrease in eye contact may be one of the very first signs of autism, and can begin as early as at two months old. Eye contact is present but in decline in two- to six-month-old infants later diagnosed with autism. This simple but essential interaction is so noticeable because its lack makes us uncomfortable. It's hard for most of us to trust someone who won't make eye contact.

But sometimes people with completely intact ToM turn it off because they just don't *want* to know what someone else is thinking or feeling about them. Many of my most abused patients—people who have suffered physical, sexual, and emotional abuse—have great difficulty making eye contact. Other examples were documented by a group of Canadian researchers. They discovered that women who were abused as children appear to have unconsciously inhibited their ability to use ToM. In particular, they have difficulty interpreting family interactions and are slower to recognize what others are thinking or feeling in general. Why would they want to know how other people see them if they've already decided that what those people would see would be of such little value? So they either shut down their ToM, or they turn it way up, misinterpreting the slightest gesture, tone of voice, or innocent remark negatively as a self-fulfilling prophecy of their lack of worth.

This is just some of the compelling evidence of how early childhood parenting and experiences influence brain development. A lot of that influence has to do with the amount of the "feel-good hormone," oxytocin, in the brain. When children with autism are given extra oxytocin, they get better at ToM. Oxytocin has recently been implicated in the growth and development of mirror neurons, that brain tool involved in mirroring the emotions of another person.

From my experience as a psychiatrist, a disruption in ToM can have unforeseen and negative consequences. Because we all expect another person to have an intact ToM, and therefore be interested in what we think or feel, people impaired in this area can appear insensitive and uncaring. In response, people with an intact ToM may then activate their own limbic system—the seat of emotions—feeling angry, anxious, or useless. People caring for trauma victims, and those diagnosed with borderline personality disorder, may have felt these emotions. The doctors and nurses in the ER did when Sheila arrived with self-inflicted wounds. When giving care to someone who's oblivious to his or her own impacts, it helps to know that the person isn't being oppositional on purpose. Reactivating our own ToM can help us reach out to them in a more empathetic and therapeutic way, just as we would to someone with dementia or autism.

▶ **OPEN A BOOK AND YOU'LL FIND THEORY OF MIND**

"It's in literature that true life can be found. It's under the mask of fiction that you can tell the truth," wrote Nobel-winning novelist Gao Xingjian. When it comes to exercising or strengthening our ToM abilities, it turns out that reading fiction can give you an edge. In a number of recent studies, researchers showed that reading fiction actually improved ToM. Fiction, they believe, "provides an opportunity to simulate the character's social experience and thus provide a forum for the reader to practice reasoning about others' mental states." It helps readers "build social knowledge by exposing them to social rules and contingencies presented in the context of the story."

According to other research at the New School for Social Research, not all fiction is the same. In five varied experiments, a group studied ToM scores among subjects reading different types of literature. They found that reading literary fiction led to higher scores than reading popular fiction or nonfiction.

If reading fiction does indeed improve ToM ability, perhaps this could be considered a simple, affordable, and enjoyable method of helping boost the skills of those in need. And it's not a bad idea for the rest of us to read more too.

THE SURMOUNTABLE PAST

The home domain is truly powerful in helping us all form trusting relationships and a sense of value. How we raise our children, and the home and social environments we create for them, can have a direct influence on how well they develop Theory of Mind. The more valuable we make children feel, the more adept they become at recognizing people's thoughts and feelings and responding appropriately to elicit an anticipated reaction.

For those whose Theory of Mind has been turned off as a coping method for past abuse and neglect, the road back to trust and a more functional ToM may take longer. This can be the case especially when parents use "love withdrawal" as a way to discipline their children, and it's a parenting style that sadly gets passed down the generations that I see too much of still. For example, let's look at a patient of mine and his chaotic and volatile relationship with his mother.

Raphael told me the story of a time when he was six years old and had made his three-year-old cousin cry. His mother, furious and trying to discipline him, told him she didn't love him because of what he had done. She said this regularly when he misbehaved, and those words echo in his ears even now as an adult so that he isn't able to trust his mother.

In essence, such parents use alienation to send a message that a behavior is not acceptable. This is the parent who responds, "No you're not" when the child says "I'm hungry," thus invalidating the child's experience and leaving the developing brain confused. This is the parent who says "I don't care" when a child seeks comfort. In response, the child cries louder, and feels abandoned even when the parent is sitting right there.

In fascinating research done at Leiden University in the Netherlands, scientists took fifty-four women who reported varying degrees of being disciplined by alienation as children and had them participate in a virtual ball-tossing game called Cyberball. Some of the virtual players were purposefully excluded, measured by the ball being tossed to them less often than to another player. When the subject women were given a nasal spray of oxytocin, some of them began to throw the ball more to the excluded players. The results, however, were disturbing. This increase in ball tossing was only done by those women who reported more supportive families and less discipline by love-withdrawal. The implication? Even oxytocin may not be enough to overcome early childhood experiences of feeling unloved and rejected.

However, from my professional experience, I truly believe the influence of negative experiences in the home domain is not insurmountable. Over time, and in a supportive, respectful environment, especially while using the I-M Approach, most of my patients have been able to rekindle their sense of personal value and are more willing to include other people in their lives and group, rather than excluding or creating situations in which they themselves are excluded.

It's also critical to remember that it's never too late to make new ties and build connections in life. The home domain doesn't have to loom so large as we grow into adulthood and are able to allow our place in our community and workplace (the social domain) to take a larger role in our self-perception. It turns out that even if our home domains weren't ideal, spending more of our time and energy in the wider social domain and fostering new friendships actually help us live longer. Those were indeed the findings in a ten-year longevity study of people aged seventy and older that was conducted by researchers at the Centre for Ageing Studies at Flinders University in Adelaide, Australia. The report was based on a series of interviews of 1,500 older people, tracking them over ten years. The researchers took other factors into consideration such as economic, social, environmental, and lifestyle habits. After controlling for this wide variety of circumstances, the team was able to pinpoint the positive effect friendships have on longevity. Other findings of the research are intriguing.

- Close relationships with children and relatives had little effect on longevity rates for older people during the ten-year study.
- People with extensive networks of good friends and confidantes outlived those with the fewest friends by 22 percent.

- The positive effects of friendships on longevity continued throughout the decade, regardless of other profound life changes such as the death of a spouse or other close family members.

One of the study authors, Lynne Giles, brings home the point, especially as it relates to building connections, when she said in an interview on the Centre's website:

> The central message is that maintaining a sense of social embedded-ness through friends and family appears pretty important for survival and it seems that non-kin relationships are particularly important.

So what I tell all my patients is that every friend was once a stranger. The reason they and we remain strangers is that we worry they will judge us negatively, and they worry that we will judge them negatively. We are using ToM all the time, trying to understand each other, and trying (needing) to make a connection.

 Exercise

STOP, LOOK, AND LISTEN

As you now know, we can use ToM to build someone up or tear someone down. Your influence is up to you. A person who has a sense of value is a person more likely to reciprocate value, while a person you've devalued is more likely to retaliate. Knowing the mechanism of this influence, you now can make a conscious effort to increase other people's own value and membership in the group. You can try this with strangers. It can be as simple as offering a smile, saying "good morning" when you step on the elevator, or holding open a door, and apologizing if you forgot to hold it. With people you already know, the exchange happening with ToM can be pretty easy, as you value each other already.

But how about someone you've had a difficult relationship

with? That can be trickier. If indeed you'd like to shift the relationship from alienation to membership, then I have an exercise for you.

It's called "Stop, Look, and Listen." Pick a person with whom you have a conflict. Before talking with them, use what you know about Theory of Mind and the I-M Approach to assess

1. how you *think* they feel about you,
2. what you *want* them to think and feel about you,
3. how you feel about them, and
4. how you think they think you feel about them.

Got that? But watch out. This recursive thinking can, of course, go on forever! Before that happens, go on to the next step.

Create an opportunity to speak with the person. Give them the choice of time, as it sends a message of respect. Show up a little earlier than the agreed upon time, again demonstrating respect. By stopping what you are doing to pay attention to the person, you also increase their value. Remember that respect leads to value, so you have immediately begun to change the perception of that person from alienation to membership.

Take care to make eye contact, which indicates you are not a threat. And then listen to what the person has to say, talk *with* them, not *to* them, which lowers the person's anxiety. Remember, anxiety is a form of stress, and the response to stress is fight-flight-freeze. You now have an opportunity to create that connection, and perhaps even friendship. Use your prefrontal cortex to anticipate the consequence of membership compared to alienation. You are sending a message to the other person's brain that they are respected and valued; this then leads to trust, the cardinal ingredient to sustained membership in a group. You have taken a next natural step in our human evolution exercising your awareness and understanding of Theory of Mind.

BUILDING HEALTH WITH ToM
(BECAUSE IT'S GOOD FOR YOU)

What most of the older people in the Australian longevity study noted above would likely tell you is exactly what you've learned by reading these pages: being connected and part of a group increases your sense of being valued, and value leads to trust. Not surprisingly, being valued generates a feeling of pleasure, a critical role in conjunction with ToM as a positive reinforcement of social connection. And it is once again oxytocin that is at work here. But it's a neurohormone that you can build more of through connection.

Behavioral scientists at Cedars-Sinai Medical Center in Los Angeles conducted a review of 102 articles about oxytocin published between 1959 and 2009. They concluded that oxytocin induced "a general sense of well-being including calm, improved social interactions, increased trust, and reduced fear." Simple things like touch and the perception of emotional support trigger the release of this "trust hormone" in the brain. Its broader influence, however, is on physical health, as oxytocin has even been shown to reduce blood pressure.

In one recent study, scientists from Brigham Young University measured the oxytocin and cortisol (the chemical associated with stress) in thirty-four married couples over four weeks. Couples that exchanged more warm touches had more oxytocin, less cortisol, and lower blood pressure. Husbands who were given a hug by their wives in particular had lower blood pressure than those who did not receive hugs from their wives. That warm touch indicated social and emotional support, interpreted through our ability to use ToM with a partner. In contrast, other important brain research tells us that a dysfunction of oxytocin and its receptors appears related to conditions like anxiety, autism, and even schizophrenia.

But you don't have to be married to build connection and create more oxytocin for yourself and others. There are many people who focus on the well-being of others and the community at large and thereby create wells of oxytocin for everyone.

* * *

REGGIE: A LOVE STORY

Reggie was small in stature but giant in spirit. Around his small and sleepy town he was easily identified by his bowler hat. He was a noble and gallant fellow in his late fifties, a master carpenter and the face of friendship. For more than two decades each Christmas season, he had dressed up in a custom-made Santa suit for town gatherings. His house sparkled with the peaceful glow of colored lights, cherubs and seraphim, candles in windows, and the promise of Christmas.

One year a large wooden box, more than six feet tall and just as wide, had appeared on his lawn. It looked like an enormous present—a nice addition to the holiday theme.

No one had any idea that something was actually inside.

And then, on Christmas Day, in his Santa suit, in front of a few neighbors, Reggie had opened the box. There, in full regalia, shiny black paint contrasted with reds and whites, yellows and blues was a wooden soldier. The soldier's tall hat was adorned with the town seal—Reggie had made the town a Christmas toy.

Each year after that Reggie repeated his gift giving. A new box would appear on Reggie's lawn, and the town would speculate on what was in it. On Christmas Day, Santa would once again emerge and open the box. One year Reggie carved a beautiful angel. Another year, a sled. And for several years various reindeer, elves, and other festive sculptures—all carved with love and care. Each of Reggie's carvings became part of the civic decorations. Reggie repeated the joy in giving, both for himself and for the recipients. Hundreds, if not thousands, were touched in some way by Reggie's gifts.

But then Reggie became wracked with arthritis, and he could no longer hold his carpentry tools without pain. He stopped working, couldn't pay his mortgage, and the bank was foreclosing on his home. Reggie felt hopeless, helpless, and worthless. People began to notice he wasn't around as much. More than having lost his monetary worth, Reggie felt he had no value to anyone, increasingly crippled by the body that was betraying him.

His friends became concerned about the change. In response, they organized a tribute and fundraiser at the local Knights of Columbus Hall. One hundred people, many of whom were strangers personally to Reggie, but who knew of his contributions to the town, gathered to honor him and to see if they could help. Reggie basked in the glow and the warmth he felt from his community, his eyes filling with tears. As Reggie described the event later, he likened it to the classic film *It's a Wonderful Life*, which championed the belief that good deeds will be rewarded. For years Reggie had treated his community with value. And when he needed it most, his community had reciprocated, reminding Reggie that no matter how his biological domain was wracked with arthritis he was and would always be a valued member of the town.

* * *

As Reggie's story shows, we all have something to give. We all have the capacity to connect, no matter what our circumstances or the current state of our four domains: biological, Ic, home, and social. Throughout our lives, each of us is at an I-M, doing the best we can in each moment. By fine-tuning our Theory of Mind to further value and respect ourselves and others, we have the potential to build the trust that takes our I-M to ever-more rewarding levels.

Your knowledge and application of ToM can help influence others' perceptions of you and give them the opportunity to really "get" you, as you allow yourself to really "get" them. Not everyone will always see you for who you really are, nor will you always be fully present to others. But the possibility for connection is truly endless.

Include or exclude? You get to choose. At every moment you have an opportunity to remind someone of their value, or to devalue them. You control no one and influence everyone. What kind of influence do you want to be? How do you want people to really get you? What small change do you want to make today, right now, to take your I-M to the next potential?

Do you get me?

REFERENCES

Chapter 1

Acher, R., "Molecular evolution of neurohypophyseal hormones and neurophysins." *Neurosecretion and Neuroendocrine Activity*, 1978, 31–43.

Bar, Moshe, Maital Neta, and Heather Linz. "Very first impressions." *Emotion* 6, no. 2 (May 2006): 269–78.

Bastiaansen, J. A. C. J., Thioux, M., Keysers, C. "Evidence for mirror systems in emotions." *Philosophical Transactions of the Royal Society B* 364, no. 1528 (2009): 2391–404.

Baron-Cohen, Simon, Michelle O'Riordan, Valarie Stone, Rosie Jones, and Kate Plaisted. "Recognition of faux pas by normally developing children and children with Asperger syndrome or high-functioning autism." *Journal of Autism and Developmental Disorders* 29, no. 5 (1999): 407–18.

Becchio, Cristina, Andrea Cavallo, Chiara Begliomini, Luisa Sartori, Giampietro Feltrin, and Umberto Castiello. "Social grasping: From mirroring to mentalizing." *NeuroImage* 61, no. 1 (2012): 240–48.

Bosch, Oliver J., and Inga D. Neumann. "Both oxytocin and vasopressin are mediators of maternal care and aggression in rodents: From central release to site of action." *Hormones and Behavior* 61, no. 3 (2012): 293–303.

Brunnlieb, Claudia, Thomas F. Münte, Claus Tempelmann, and Marcus Heldmann. "Vasopressin modulates neural responses related to emotional stimuli in the right amygdala." *Brain Research* 1499 (March 2013): 29–42.

Carter, C. Sue. "Oxytocin pathways and the evolution of human behavior." *Annual Review of Psychology* 65 (January 2014): 17–39.

Corballis, Michael C. "Mirror neurons and the evolution of language." *Brain and Language* 112, no. 1 (January 2010): 25–35.

de Souza, Alzira Martins Ferreira, and Jorge A. López. "Insulin or insulin-like studies on unicellular organisms: A review." *Brazilian Archives of Biology and Technology* 47, no. 6 (November 2004): 973–81.

Donaldson, Zoe R., and Young, Larry J. "Oxytocin, vasopressin, and the neurogenetics of sociality." *Science* 322, no. 5903 (2008): 900–904.

Gruber, Christian W. "Physiology of invertebrate oxytocin and vasopressin neuropeptides." *Experimental Physiology* 99, no. 1 (January 2014): 55–61.

Gweon, Hyowon, David Dodell-Feder, Marina Bedny, and Rebecca Saxe. "Theory of mind performance in children correlates with functional specialization of a brain region for thinking about thoughts. *Child Development* 83, no. 6 (November/December 2012): 1853–68.

Hammock, Elizabeth A. D. "Developmental perspectives on oxytocin and vasopressin." *Neuropsychopharmacology* 40, no. 1 (January 2015): 24–42.

Isoda, Masaki, and Atsushi Noritake. "What makes the dorsomedial frontal cortex active during reading the mental states of others?" *Frontiers in Neuroscience* 7 no. 232 (December 5, 2013).

Knobloch, H. Sophie, and Valery Grinevich. "Evolution of oxytocin pathways in the brain of vertebrates." *Frontiers in Behavioral Neuroscience* 8, no. 31 (2014).

Lee, Heon-Jin, Abbe H. Macbeth, Jerome Pagani, W. Scott Young 3rd. "Oxytocin: The great facilitator of life." *Progress in Neurobiology* 88, no. 2 (June 2009): 127–51.

Litvin, Yoav, Gen Murakami, and Donald W. Pfaff. "Effects of chronic social defeat on behavioral and neural correlates of sociality: Vasopressin, oxytocin and the vasopressinergic V1b receptor." *Physiology & Behavior* 103, no. 3–4 (June 2011) 393–403.

Lukas, Michael, and Inga D. Neumann. "Oxytocin and vasopressin in rodent behaviors related to social dysfunctions in autism spectrum disorders." *Behavioural Brain Research* 251 (August 2013): 85–94.

Marrus, Natasha, Anne L. Glowinski, Theodore Jacob, Ami Klin, Warren Jones, Caroline E. Drain, Kieran E. Holzhauer, et al. "Rapid video-referenced ratings of reciprocal social behavior in toddlers: A twin study." *Journal of Child Psychology and Psychiatry* (February 18, 2015).

Moore, Frank L. "Evolutionary precedents for behavioral actions of oxytocin and vasopressin. *Annals of the New York Academy of Science* 652 (June 1992): 156–65.

Nielsen, Mark. "Imitation, pretend play, and childhood: Essential elements in the evolution of human culture?" *Journal of Comparative Psychology* 126, no. 2 (May 2012): 170–81.

Neumann, Inga D. "The advantage of social living: Brain neuropeptides mediate the beneficial consequences of sex and motherhood." *Frontiers in Neuroendocrinology* 30, no. 4 (October 2009): 483–96.

Premack, David, and Guy Woodruff. "Does the chimpanzee have a theory of mind?" *Behavioral Brain Sciences* 1, no. 4 (December 1978): 515–26.

Ramsey, Richard, and Antonia F. de C. Hamilton. "How does your own knowledge influence the perception of another person's action in the human brain?" *Social Cognitive and Affective Neuroscience* 7, no. 2 (February 2012): 242–51.

Restak, Richard. "Fixing the brain." *Mysteries of the Mind*. Washington, DC: National Geographic Society, 2000.

Saxe, R., and N. Kanwisher. "People thinking about thinking people: The role of the temporo-parietal junction in 'theory of mind.'" *NeuroImage* 19 (2003): 1835–42.

Sebastian, Lucille T., Lisa De Matteo, Geoffrey Shaw, and Marilyn B. Renfree. "Mesotocin receptors during pregnancy, parturition and lactation in the tammar wallaby." *Animal Reproduction Science* 57, no. 1 (1998) 57–74.

Seyfarth, Robert, and Dorothy L. Cheney. "Affiliation, empathy, and the origins of theory of mind." *Proceedings of the National Academy of Sciences in the United States of America* 110, suppl. 2 (June 2013): 10349–56.

Uzefovskym, Florina, Idan Shalev, Salomon Israel, Ariel Knafo, and Richard P. Ebstein. "Vasopressin selectively impairs emotion recognition in men." *Psychoneuroendocrinology* 37, no. 4 (April 2012): 576–80.

Viero, Cedric, Izumi Shibuya, Naoki Kitamura, Alexei Verkhratsky, Kiroaki Fujihara, Akiko Katoh, Yoichi Ueta, et al. "Oxytocin: Crossing the bridge between basic science and pharmacotherapy." *CNS Neuroscience & Therapeutics* 16, no. 5 (October 2010): e138–56.

Wimmer, Hanz, and Josef Perner. "Beliefs about beliefs: Representation and constraining function of wrong beliefs in young children's understanding of deception." *Cognition* 13, no. 1 (January 1983): 103–28.

Chapter 2

"Be Kind; Everyone You Meet Is Fighting a Hard Battle." Quote Investigator, June 29, 2010, http://quoteinvestigator.com/2010 /06/29/be-kind/.

Birch, Cheryl D., Brad R. C. Kelln, and Emmanuel P. B. Aquino. "A review and case report of pseudologia fantastica." *The Journal of Forensic Psychiatry & Psychology* 17 no. 2 (June 2006): 299–320.

Dobrila-Dintinjana, R., and A. Nacinović-Duletić. "Placebo in the treatment of pain." *Collegium Antropologicum* 35, Suppl. 2 (September 2011): 319–23.

du Saint-Exupéry, Antoine. *The Little Prince*. Paris: Gallimard, 1943.

Evans, Angela D., and Kang Lee. "Emergence of lying in very young children." *Developmental Psychology* 49, no. 10 (October 2013): 1958–63.

Evans, Angela D., and Kang Lee. "Promising to tell the truth makes 8- to 16-year-olds more honest." *Behavioral Science & the Law* 28, no. 6 (November/December 2010): 801–11.

Finney, Jack. *Time and Again*. New York: Simon and Schuster, 1970.

Gold, Azgad, and Pesach Lichtenberg. "The moral case for the clinical placebo." *Journal of Medical Ethics* 40 (2014): 219–24.

Hays, Chelsea, and Leslie J. Carver. "Follow the liar: The effects of adult lies on children's honesty." *Developmental Science* 17, no. 6 (November 2014): 977–83.

Henriques, Diana B. "Madoff is sentenced to 150 years for ponzi scheme." *New York Times,* June 29, 2009, www.nytimes.com/2009 /06/30/business/30madoff.html?_r=0.

Lewis, Michael, Catherine Stanger, and Margaret W. Sullivan. "Deception in 3-year-olds." *Developmental Psychology* 25, no. 3 (1989): 439–43.

Rosenberg, Eric. "U.S. internet fraud at all-time high."*San Francisco Chronicle,* March 31, 2007, www.sfgate.com/crime/article/U-S -Internet-fraud-at-all-time-high-Nigerian-2576989.php.

Serota, Kim, Timothy R. Levine, and Franklin J. Boster. "The prevalence of lying in America: Three studies of self-reported lies." *Human Communication Research* 36 (2010): 2–25.

Chapter 3

Andréasson, Sven, Anna-Karin Danielsson, and Sara Wallhed-Finn. "Preferences regarding treatment for alcohol problems." *Alcohol and Alcoholism* 48, no. 6 (November 2013): 694–9.

Amdurer, Emily, Richard E. Boyatzis, Argun Saatcioglu, Melvin L. Smith, Scott N. Taylor. "Long term impact of emotional, social and cognitive intelligence competencies and GMAT on career and life satisfaction and career success." *Frontiers in Psychology* 5 (December 2014): 1447.

Azevedo, Ruben T., Emiliano Macaluso, Alessio Avenanti, Valerio Santangelo, Valentina Cazzato, and Salvatore Maria Aglioti. "Their pain is not our pain: Brain and autonomic correlates of empathic resonance with the pain of same and different race individuals." *Human Brain Mapping* 34, no. 12 (December 2013): 3168–81.

Burris, Jessica L., Amy E. Wahlquist, and Matthew J. Carpenter. "Characteristics of cigarette smokers who want to quit now versus quit later." *Addictive Behavior* 38, no. 6 (June 2013): 2257–60.

Curtis, John M., and Mimi J. Curtis. "Factors related to susceptibility and recruitment by cults." *Psychological Reports* 73 (1993): 451–60.

Egley, Arlen Jr., James C. Howell, and Meena Harris. "Highlights of the 2012 National Youth Gang Survey." *Office of Juvenile Justice and Delinquency Prevention.* (December 2014): 2.

Goleman, Daniel, *Emotional Intelligence: Why It Can Matter More Than IQ.* New York: Bantam Books, 1995.

Gouin, Jean-Philippe, C. Sue Carter, Hossein Pournajafi-Nazarloo, Ronald Glaser, William B. Malarkey, Timothy J. Loving, Jeffrey Stowell, and Janice K. Kiecolt-Glaser. "Marital behavior, oxytocin, vasopressin, and wound healing." *Psychoneuroendocrinology* 35, no. 7 (August 2010): 1082–90.

Kapogiannis, Dimitrios, Gopikrishna Deshpande, Frank Krueger, Matthew P. Thornburg, Jordan Henry Grafman. "Brain networks shaping religious belief." *Brain Connectivity* 4, no. 1 (February 2014): 70–79.

Lee, Eunju J. "Differential susceptibility to the effects of child temperament on maternal warmth and responsiveness." *Journal of Genetic Psychology* 174, no. 4 (2013): 429–49.

Lewis-Morrarty, Erin, Mary Dozier, Kristin Bernard, Stephanie Terracciano, and Shannon Moore. "Cognitive flexibility and Theory of Mind outcomes among foster children: Preschool follow-up results of a randomized clinical trial." *Journal of Adolescent Health* 51, suppl. 2 (August 2012): S17–22.

Lindner, Isabel, Cécile Schain, René Kopietz, and Gerald Echterhoff. "When do we confuse self and other in action memory? Reduced false memories of self-performance after observing actions by an out-group vs. in-group actor." *Frontiers in Psychology* 3, no. 467 (2012).

Mehler, K., D. Wendrich, R. Kissgen, B. Roth, A. Oberthuer, F. Pillekamp, and A. Kribs. "Mothers seeing their VLBW infants within 3 h after birth are more likely to establish a secure attachment behavior: Evidence of a sensitive period with preterm infants?" Journal of Perinatology 31 (June 2011): 404–10.

Misch, Antonia, Harriet Over, and Malinda Carpenter. "Stick with your group: Young children's attitudes about group loyalty." *Journal of Experimental Child Psychology* 126 (October 2014): 19–36.

Molenberghs, Pascal, Veronika Halász, Jason B. Mattingley, Eric J. Vanman, and Ross Cunnington. "Seeing is believing: Neural mechanisms of action-perception are biased by team membership." *Human Brain Mapping* 34, no. 9 (September 2013): 2055–68.

Morrison, Samantha, Jean Decety, and Pascal Molenberghs. "The neuroscience of group membership." *Neuropsychologia* 50, no. 8 (July 2012): 2114–20.

Pew Forum on Religion & Public Life. "'Nones' on the Rise: One-in-Five Adults Have No Religious Affiliation." Pew Research Center, October 2012, www.pewforum.org/files/2012/10/NonesOnTheRise-full.pdf.

Robinson, Beth, Ellen M. Frye, and Loretta J. Bradley. "Cult affiliation and disaffiliation: Implications for counseling." *Counseling and Values* 41, no. 2 (January 1997):166–73.

Rubie-Davies, Christine M. "Teacher expectations and perceptions of student attributes: Is there a relationship?" *British Journal of Educational Psychology* 80, no. 1 (March 2010): 121–35.

Scheele, Dirk, Andrea Wille, Keith M. Kendrick, Birgit Stoffel-Wagner, Benjamin Becker, Onur Güntürkün, Wolfgamg Maier, and René Hulemann. "Oxytocin enhances brain reward system responses in men viewing the face of their female partner." *Proceedings of the National Academy of Sciences of the United States of America* 110, no. 50 (December 2013): 20308–13.

Solovieva, Tatiana I., Denetta L. Dowler, and Richard T. Walls. "Employer benefits from making workplace accommodations." *Disability and Health Journal* 4, no. 1 (January 2011): 39–45.

Thornberry, Terence P. "Membership in Youth Gangs and Involvement in Serious and Violent Offending." In *Serious and Violent Juvenile Offenders: Risk Factors and Successful Interventions*, edited by Rolf Loeber and David P. Farrington, 147–66. Thousand Oaks, CA: Sage Publications, Inc., 1998.

Chapter 4

Anthes, Emily. "Their pain, our gain: Why schadenfreude is best enjoyed in groups." *Scientific American,* November/December 2010, www.scientificamerican.com/article/their-pain-our-gain/.

Barry, Heather, and Tom R. Tyler. "The other side of injustice: When unfair procedures increase group-serving behavior." *Psychological Science* 20, no. 8 (August 2009): 1026–32.

Bick, Johanna, Victoria Nguyen, Lin Leng, Marta Piecychna, Michael J. Crowley, Richard Bucala, Linda C. Mayes, and Ellen L. Grigorenko. "Preliminary associations between childhood neglect, MIF, and cortisol: Potential pathways to long-term disease risk." *Developmental Psychobiology* 57, no. 1 (January 2015): 131–39.

Bridgman, Matthew W., Warren S. Brown, Michael L. Spezio, Matthew K. Leonard, Ralph Adolphs, and Lynn K. Paul. "Facial emotion recognition in agenesis of the corpus callosum." *Journal of Neurodevelopmental Disorders* 6, no. 32 (2014): 32.

Carroll, Judith E., Tara L. Gruenwald, Shelley E. Taylor, Denise Janicki-Deverts, Karen A. Matthews, and Teresa E. Seeman. "Childhood abuse, parental warmth, and adult multisystem biological risk in the Coronary Artery Risk Development in Young Adults study." *Proceedings of the National Academy of Sciences* 110, no. 42 (October 15, 2013).

Choi, Jeewook, Bumseok Jeong, Michael L. Rohan, Ann M. Polcari, Martin H. Teicher. "Preliminary evidence for white matter tract abnormalities in young adults exposed to parental verbal abuse." *Biological Psychiatry* 65, no. 3 (February 1, 2009): 227–34.

De Dreu, Carsten K. W. "Oxytocin modulates cooperation within and competition between groups: An integrative review and research agenda." *Hormones and Behavior* 61, no. 3 (March 2012): 419–28.

Egas, Martijn, Ralph Kats, Xander van der Sar, Ernesto Reuben, and Maurice W. Sabelis. "Human cooperation by lethal group competition." *Scientific Reports* 3, no. 1373 (March 2013).

Fiske, Susan T. "Varieties of (de) humanization: Divided by competition and status." *Nebraska Symposium on Motivation* 60 (2013): 53–71.

Fu, Genyue, Angela D. Evans, Lingfeng Wang, and Kang Lee. "Lying in the name of the collective good: A developmental study." *Developmental Science* 11, no. 4 (July 2008): 495–503.

Glowacki, Luke, and Richard E. Wrangham. "The role of rewards in motivating participation in simple warfare." *Human Nature* 24, no. 4 (December 2013): 444–60.

Gneezy, Ayelet, and Daniel M. T. Fessler. "Conflict, sticks and carrots: War increases prosocial punishments and rewards." *Proceedings of the Royal Society B* 279 (2012): 219–23.

Josephson, Eric, and Mary Josephson. *Man Alone: Alienation in Modern Society.* New York: Dell Publishing Co., 1977, 16.

Laslett, Peter. *The World We Have Lost: Further Explored*, 4th ed. England: Routledge, 2005, 93.

Lewandowsky, Stephan, Werner G. K. Stritzke, Alexandra M. Freund, Klaus Oberauer, and Joachim I. Krueger. "Misinformation, disinformation, and violent conflict: From Iraq and the 'War on Terror' to future threats to peace." *American Psychologist* 68, no. 7 (October 2013): 487–501.

Marks, Johnny. "Rudolph the Red-Nosed Reindeer." Song from 1939.

Shakoor, Sania, Sara R. Jaffee, Lucy Bowes, Isabelle Ouellet-Morin, Penelope Andreou, Francesca Happé, Terrie E. Moffitt, and Louise Arseneault. "A prospective longitudinal study of children's Theory of Mind and adolescent involvement in bullying." *Journal of Child Psychology and Psychiatry* 53, no. 3 (March 2012): 254–61.

Spielmann, Stephanie S., Geoff MacDonald, Jessica A. Maxwell, Samantha Joel, Diana Peragine, Amy Muise, and Emily A. Impett. "Settling for less out of fear of being single." *Journal of Personality and Social Psychology* 105, no. 6 (December 2013): 1049–73.

Sutton, J., P. K. Smith, and J. Swettenham. "Social cognition and bullying: Social inadequacy or skilled manipulation?" *British Journal of Developmental Psychology* 14, no. 3 (September 1999): 435–50.

Teicher, Martin H., Jacqueline A. Samson, Yi-Shin Sheu, Ann Polcari, and Cynthia E. McGreenery. "Hurtful words: Association of exposure to peer verbal abuse with elevated psychiatric symptom scores and corpus callosum abnormalities." *American Journal of Psychiatry* 167, no. 12 (December 2010): 1464–71.

Volk, Anthony A., Joseph A. Camilleri, Andrew V. Dane, and Zopito A. Marini. "Is adolescent bullying an evolutionary adaptation?" *Aggressive Behavior* 38, no. 3 (May/June 2012): 222–38.

Chapter 5

Agroskin, Dmitrij, Johannes Klackl, and Eva Jonas. "The self-liking brain: A VBM study on the structural substrate of self-esteem." *PLOS One* 9, no. 1 (January 2014): e86430.

Dodell-Feder, David, Sarah Hope Lincoln, Joseph P. Coulson, and Christine I. Hooker. "Using fiction to assess mental state understanding: A new task for assessing Theory of Mind in adults." *PLoS One* 8, no. 11 (November 2013): e81279.

Fishman, Inna, Christopher L. Keown, Alan J. Lincoln, Jaime A. Pineda, Ralph-Axel Müller. "Atypical cross talk between mentalizing and mirror neuron networks in autism spectrum disorder." *JAMA Psychiatry* 71, no. 7 (2014): 751–60.

Giles, Lynne C., Gary F. V. Glonek, Mary A. Luszcz, and Gary R. Andrews. "Effect of social networks on 10 year survival in very old Australians: The Australian longitudinal study of aging." *Journal of Epidemiology and Community Health* 59 (2005): 574–79.

Holt-Lunstad, J., W. A. Birmingham, and K. C. Light. "Influence of a 'warm touch' support enhancement intervention among married couples on ambulatory blood pressure, oxytocin, alpha amylase, and cortisol." *Psychosomatic Medicine* 70, no. 9 (November 2008): 976–85.

IsHak, Waguih William, Maria Kahloon, and Hala Fakhry. "Oxytocin role in enhancing well-being: A literature review." *Journal of Affective Disorders* 130, no. 1–2 (April 2011): 1–9.

Klin, Ami, Cheryl Klaiman, and Warren Jones. "Reducing age of autism diagnosis: Developmental social neuroscience meets public health challenge." *Revista de Neurologia* 60, suppl. 1 (February 2015): S3–S11.

Moore, Thomas J., Joseph Glenmullen, and Donald R. Mattison. "Reports of pathological gambling, hypersexuality and compulsive shopping associated with dopamine receptor agonist drugs." *JAMA Internal Medicine* 174, no. 12 (2014): 1930–33.

National Association for Self-Esteem, www.self-esteem-nase.org.

Nazarov, A., P. Frewen, M. Parlar, C. Oremus, G. MacQueen, M. McKinnon, and R. Lanius. "Theory of Mind performance in women with posttraumatic stress disorder related to childhood abuse." *Acta Psychiatrica Scandinavica* 129, no. 3 (March 2014): 193–201.

Pedroni, Andreas, Christoph Eisenegger, Matthias N. Hartmann, Urs Fischbacher, and Daria Knoch. "Dopaminergic stimulation increases selfish behavior in the absence of punishment threat." *Psychopharmacology* 231, no. 1 (January 2014): 135–41.

Riem, Madelon M. E., Marian J. Bakermans-Kranenburg, Renske Huffmeijer, Marinus H. van Ijzendoorn. "Does intranasal oxytocin promote prosocial behavior to an excluded fellow player? A randomized-controlled trial with Cyberball." *Psychoneuroendocrinology* 38, no. 8 (August 2013): 1418–25.

Singh, Minati. "Mood, food, and obesity." *Frontiers in Psychology* 5, no. 925 (September 1, 2014).

Somerville, Leah H., William M. Kelley, and Todd F. Heatherton. "Self-esteem modulates medial prefrontal cortical responses to evaluative social feedback." *Cerebral Cortex* 20, no. 2 (2010): 3005–13.

ABOUT THE AUTHOR

Dr. Joseph Shrand is triple board certified in adult psychiatry, child and adolescent psychiatry, and addiction medicine, and is a diplomate of the American Board of Addiction Medicine. He is also an instructor of psychiatry at Harvard Medical School and the medical director of CASTLE (Clean And Sober Teens Living Empowered), part of High Point Treatment Center in Brockton, MA.

He is the author of *Manage Your Stress: Overcoming Stress in the Modern World* and *Outsmarting Anger: 7 Strategies for Defusing Our Most Dangerous Emotion,* which was the winner of a 2013 Books for a Better Life Award in the Psychology category.

Dr. Shrand helped to design the Independence Academy, the first sober high school on the South Shore of Massachusetts, and currently sits on its steering committee. He teaches psychiatry residents-in-training as a member of the Brockton VA staff and is the medical director of Road to Responsibility, a community-based program that tends to adults with significant developmental disabilities. He is also the founder of Drug Story Theater, Inc., a nonprofit organization that teaches improvisational theater techniques to teenagers in the early stages of recovery from alcohol and other drug addictions.

"Doctor Joe," as he is affectionately called by colleagues and staff, is a nationally recognized psychiatric expert and appears regularly on New England Cable News, where he has been asked to comment on topics ranging from the Boston Marathon bombings to the Newtown tragedy. He was featured in an ABC News series during the 2012 Suicide Prevention Week, and has been quoted in popular magazines and websites such as *Good Housekeeping, Psychology Today, Everyday Health,* and TODAY's section "Today Parents."

ABOUT HAZELDEN PUBLISHING

As part of the Hazelden Betty Ford Foundation, Hazelden Publishing offers both cutting-edge educational resources and inspirational books. Our print and digital works help guide individuals in treatment and recovery, and their loved ones. Professionals who work to prevent and treat addiction also turn to Hazelden Publishing for evidence-based curricula, digital content solutions, and videos for use in schools, treatment programs, correctional programs, and electronic health records systems. We also offer training for implementation of our curricula.

Through published and digital works, Hazelden Publishing extends the reach of healing and hope to individuals, families, and communities affected by addiction and related issues.

For more information about Hazelden publications,
please call 800-328-9000
or visit us online at hazelden.org/bookstore.

OTHER TITLES THAT MAY INTEREST YOU

The Fear Reflex
Five Ways to Overcome It and Trust Your Imperfect Self

Joseph Shrand, MD, and Leigh Devine

Dr. Shrand, a leading expert on the psychology of fear, teaches us how to use the rational parts of our brains to change our perspective and respond rationally to fears as they present themselves.

Order No. 7594 (softcover), EB7594 (e-book)

The Gifts of Imperfection
*Let Go of Who You Think You're Supposed
to Be and Embrace Who You Are*

Brené Brown, PhD, LMSW

This *New York Times* best seller by Brené Brown, PhD, a leading expert on shame, blends original research with honest storytelling and helps readers move from "What will people think?" to "I am enough."

Order No. 2545 (softcover), EB2545 (e-book)

Becoming a Genuine Leader
Succeed with Integrity by Exploring Your Past

Marilyn Mason, PhD

In *Becoming a Genuine Leader,* Marilyn Mason teaches us how to lead from within by understanding our past and changing the behaviors and communication styles that have compromised our integrity.

Order No. 4136 (softcover), EB4136 (e-book)

Hazelden Publishing books are available at fine bookstores everywhere. To order from Hazelden Publishing, call 800-328-9000 or visit hazelden.org/bookstore.